C FOOD

C FOOD

ROBERT CLARK
HARRY KAMBOLIS

PHOTOGRAPHY BY HAMID ATTIE

whitecap

Whitecap Books is known for its expertise in the cookbook market,
and has produced some of the most innovative and familiar titles found in
kitchens across North America. Visit our website at www.whitecap.ca.

EDITED BY **Julia Aitken**
PROOFREAD BY **Ann-Marie Metten**
COVER AND INTERIOR DESIGN BY **Mauve Pagé**

LIBRARY AND ARCHIVES CANADA CATALOGUING IN PUBLICATION

Clark, Robert (Robert Anthony)
C food / Robert Clark and Harry Kambolis.

Includes index.
ISBN 978-1-77050-004-4

1. Cookery (Seafood). 2. Cookery (Fish). 3. Cookery. 4. C Restaurant
(Vancouver, B.C.). I. Kambolis, Harry II. Title.

TX747.C53 2009   641.6'92   C2009-902681-3

The publisher acknowledges the financial support of the Government of
Canada through the Book Publishing Industry Development Program (BPIDP)
and the Province of British Columbia through the Book Publishing Tax Credit.

09 10 11 12 13   5 4 3 2 1

CONTENTS

Though I loved to fish as a child, growing up just a few blocks from the Pacific Ocean in Victoria, I had an unreasonable but very real aversion toward eating whatever it was that I was lucky enough to catch. The trouble was always the taste. I didn't like it in the least.

I eventually learned to find joy watching others fish instead. For several weeks after school in my 11th year, I would "join" the leather-faced old men casting for lingcod on the Ogden Point breakwater, thrilled by the *bawump!* and *splash!* of the occasional swell hitting the giant concrete blocks. I'd sit there and shiver in my thin school uniform and pretend to understand Cantonese by offering sage nods whenever the fishermen called out to each other over the unrelenting din in their unfathomable vernacular. I wanted to understand the process, the relationship between the fish and the hook, and the means with which the two met.

The loathing for seafood started to ease when, as an early adolescent with tastes just beginning to "acquire," certain species of fish and shellfish became palatable (by "certain species" I mean only those that tasted like things that they really were not, and by "palatable" I mean only marginally). It was progress, yea, however glacial it may have appeared to my embarrassed parents.

From there (*there* being beer-battered haddock buttressed by salt-caked chips drenched in malt vinegar and grease) my dance card soon expanded to include oysters Rockefeller and prawn cocktails. By 18, I had sheepishly sampled lobster for the first time (loved it), and was prepped and ready by the time I found myself wanting to be in a relationship with a young woman who I'd readily allow to introduce me to sushi, lest she be affronted and my affections thwarted.

Ten years working in fine restaurants later erased all prejudices. My own retarded tastes were to be surrendered by the requirements of the job. Indeed, when I became a server at a high-end restaurant in Toronto, the chef made us *try everything* before we were allowed the privilege to serve it, the novel idea being that in order to pitch it with some measure of authority it's always wise for the pitcher to have some clue as to the flavors, textures, and techniques therein.

I thus became more and more versed in the rich and seemingly inexhaustible variety of seafoods on the many menus and daily specials that I was made to memorize. I became concerned with the freshness and point of provenance of every dish I served. I struggled to learn how to fillet a sole at the table in seconds and came to know how to shuck oysters without the terror and shame that comes with stabbing myself and bursting into repressed tears in the middle of a crowded dining room. I was—pardon the pun—*hooked*.

At 29, it was time for the big leagues of Vancouver, and my boss, one of Toronto's most iconic and well-traveled restaurateurs, gave me a list suggesting where I should apply for a comparable serving job. Once unpacked, I duly took my résumé around, and pined for a call back from the restaurant at the very top of his list. That restaurant was "C": the superlative altar to local and sustainable seafood on False Creek's seawall . . .

You see, I never got the job. They never even called me.

The abject devastation I felt when it finally dawned on me that my plan had been cruelly and callously castrated has cooled in the intervening years. As a food writer I've watched executive chef Robert Clark's star continue to ascend to something akin to "super" status, and I've certainly taken part in all the media chatter. When *Vancouver* magazine asked me to write lovely things about him to celebrate his 2009 Vancouver Magazine Green Award, rightly due for his conscientious seafood sourcing and his shepherding of the Chefs' Table Society of B.C. (the province's culinary collective), I readily complied: "For all his professional accomplishments, he's a humble, straightforward, burly fellow who picks his words with careful economy, an unpretentious sort just as at home with fishermen and farmers as he is with diners and dignitaries. Together with his charming (and equally visionary) employer, restaurateur Harry Kambolis—a leader in encouraging and adopting eco-friendly practices in his rooms—Clark has played a dominant role in making our restaurant trade a model for other cities to follow."

I try not to think of all the things Harry, Robert, and chef de cuisine Quang Dang could have taught me had I been given the opportunity to run their plates (stunningly photographed throughout these pages by Hamid Attie). Why? Because it's still too soon since I picked myself up, dusted myself off, and pieced together the life that their restaurant unknowingly rent asunder. I've long since moved on to a different career, and, mercifully, my affections for good-quality seafood haven't dimmed. Yet the soreness is still there perhaps, enough so that when Clark asked if I'd pen a foreword to this long overdue book, I didn't hesitate. *At last I will have the chance to reveal myself,* I thought. *Finally, I will have my revenge!*

Alas, the publishing world, it turns out, is neither conducive nor receptive to childish plotting, especially when the people plotted against are also doing the publishing. I'm also told that it's very bad form to persecute anyone for offering up undeserved honors. Apparently, you simply thank them for the opportunity and do as they bid. I believe I now have, and that makes the most ambitious seafood restaurant in the country and me just about even.

Bon appétit!

INTRODUCTION

Creativity, sustainability, and hospitality: These three words best describe the driving forces behind C Restaurant. All of us—the owners, the management team, the staff—are committed to giving life to these concepts. To us, C Restaurant is all about providing quality food and service, and in a way we think is truly innovative and unique.

C has always searched for its own path. And that is how we approached this cookbook. This is not a conventional cookbook. It is not a series of menus or of seasons, but of photos. These conceptual photos inspired the recipes; it was through the lens of the camera that the dishes emerged.

Today's chefs and restaurant owners seek to participate in a food culture that embraces quality, diversity, and responsibility. These are the principal guidelines. But there are always obstacles to deal with. Of course one of the biggest obstacles is the mental obstacle, when you perceive limitations where there are none.

Our strategy has been to approach a dish without any preconceived ideas, and instead discover that there are endless possibilities to explore. Creativity was the guiding force behind this project.

And second of all was the integrity of the products, the foundation on which a chef will build his reputation. We began by searching out the highest quality ingredients. This has always been our muse—what exists around us in our markets, our waters, and our fields and forest. You really don't have to look any farther than your own backyard.

Within these pages are pictures and ideas meant to inspire rather than dictate, to spark a reaction rather than demand reproduction, to instigate creativity not limit it, to provoke conversation.

The story of sustainable seafood in Vancouver is the story of C Restaurant. One cannot be told without the other. In the early years of the restaurant's history, as we began to peel back the many opaque layers that surrounded the harvesting and distribution of seafood, we began to see a connection between quality and sustainability. Some of the issues that threaten sustainability of seafood are overfishing, bycatch (what is unintentionally caught when harvesting fish), and habitat destruction. *Sustainable seafood* is harvested in a manner that ensures the long-term health and integrity of a species, and the ecosystem upon which that species relies.

Since we are a business that serves seafood exclusively, we quickly saw the need to secure and support a sustainable-seafood industry. Our first baby steps were launching something called a Sustainable Environmental Awareness (SEA) program, which involved a series of tasting menus; we donated a portion of the proceeds to the David Suzuki Foundation and its marine programs. By 1999 we found we could be both responsible and viable as a business, so we continued with a *21st Century Responsible* initiative, a phrase we coined to reflect our commitment to making our menu 100 percent environmentally responsible. In the early years it was very difficult, and sometimes it seemed impossible to circumnavigate the distribution systems in British Columbia that had been around for a very long time. If it weren't for people like Christina Burridge, who has single-handedly connected us to nearly every seafood producer we work with, we may well have not succeeded.

What was thought to be "good" and "bad" tended to be murky and confusing, but there was information available from the Living Oceans Society, the David Suzuki Foundation, and the Monterey Bay Aquariums Seafood Watch program. But being the only game in town for the longest time could be very lonely, very costly, and at times very frustrating.

The launching of the Ocean Wise program by the Vancouver Aquarium in conjunction with C was what finally encouraged local seafood suppliers to get on board with sustainable practices. Ocean Wise (www .oceanwisecanada.org) is a conservation program that was created to educate and empower consumers about the issues surrounding sustainable seafood. When you see the Ocean Wise symbol on a restaurant menu or a market's display case, you know you are making an environmentally friendly choice. This program also works with restaurants to ensure that they have up-to-date and accurate information with which to make better buying choices. The success of the program can be seen today with the number of restaurants, culinary schools, markets, and suppliers participating in ongoing promotion and education.

C Restaurant seeks to provide "ethical luxury," not opulence at any cost. And above all, C is about sharing our love of food with our guests. An evening in our dining room overlooking the water on Vancouver's beautiful False Creek is an experience you won't forget. As an extension of our restaurant, we hope you enjoy this book. C is ethical luxury at its best. Enjoy.

STARTERS, SOUPS & SALADS

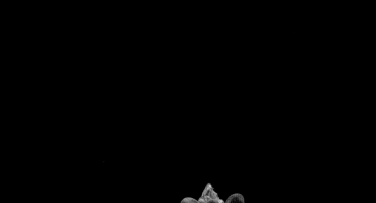
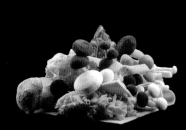

OYAMA CURED MEATS
pickled fresh figs | toasted walnuts | Farm House blue cheese panna cotta

Being part of a community means supporting that community. In and around Vancouver we are fortunate to have a vibrant group of artisan food producers who elevate the quality of products available to us all. Knowing the provenance of the products you work with is one of the cornerstones of creating wonderful food.

No one I know invests more passion in his chosen profession than Jan Driessen van der Lieck (known by many as John) at Oyama Sausage Company on Granville Island in Vancouver. His knowledge and commitment, and the consistency and quality of his cured meats and sausages, have earned him the respect of myself and other Vancouver restaurateurs. Whether playing a supporting role in soups and sauces, or starring in our plowman's lunch, you will always find an Oyama product on our menus.

Then there is the wonderful couple at The Farm House Natural Cheeses. For her handcrafted cheeses, Debra uses the milk from the cows and goats raised on their farm by her husband, George. This homegrown understanding and appreciation of the raw ingredients is the key to the quality, consistency, and success of their products, and no trip to Agassiz would be complete without a stop at their farm gate.

SERVES 6 | SERVE WITH TAVEL ROSÉ

NOTE   Start preparing this recipe at least two weeks in advance to allow time for the figs to pickle.

PICKLED FIGS
2 pounds fresh figs
4 cups white wine vinegar
4 cups water
¼ cup granulated sugar
¼ cup kosher salt
2 tablespoons anise seeds
2 pods star anise

FARM HOUSE BLUE CHEESE PANNA COTTA
12 ounces Farm House Castle
    Blue cheese or other semisoft
    blue cheese
1¼ cups whipping cream (35%)
4 sheets gelatin or 1 tablespoon
    unflavored powdered gelatin

OYAMA CURED MEAT
12 ounces artisan-produced
    cured meats (choose a
    selection, such as dry-cured
    pork, salami, and pâté)
Toasted walnuts for garnish

6

CONTINUED ON PAGE 9 . . .

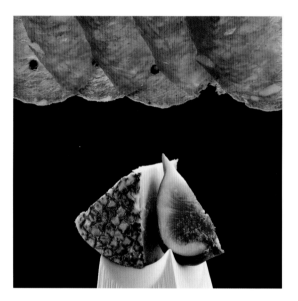

OYAMA CURED MEATS (*continued*)

1 To prepare the pickled figs, put the figs in a nonreactive bowl. Combine the remaining ingredients in a large nonreactive saucepan and bring to a boil over high heat. Pour over the figs, cover, and allow to macerate in a cool, dark spot for at least 2 weeks.

2 To prepare the Farm House blue cheese panna cotta, dice 3 ounces of the cheese and refrigerate. Into the top of a double boiler, crumble the remaining cheese and add 1 cup of the cream. Heat over medium-low heat, stirring until melted and smooth. Do not allow the mixture to get too hot.

3 In a small saucepan, heat the remaining cream over medium heat until steaming. Temper the gelatin sheets by placing them in a bowl of cold water for 2 minutes to soften. Squeeze out the excess water. Stir the soaked gelatin into the hot cream until it is completely melted. If using powdered gelatin, put 2 tablespoons cold water in a small bowl and sprinkle the gelatin over the surface. Let stand for 5 minutes or until puffy. Put the bowl in a small saucepan containing enough barely simmering water to come halfway up the sides of the bowl. Stir for 1 minute or until the gelatin is completely melted.

4 Whisk the hot cream into the gelatin. Whisk the gelatin mixture into the cheese mixture and remove from the heat. Stirring constantly, let the mixture cool to room temperature, then stir in the diced cheese. Divide evenly among six ½-cup ramekins and refrigerate overnight until set.

5 To serve, set 1 blue cheese panna cotta on each of 6 plates. Arrange the cured meats and pickled figs alongside.

9

STONEY PARADISE HEIRLOOM TOMATO SALAD

Golden Olive Eleni extra virgin olive oil | smoked sea salt flakes

---

First-rate extra virgin olive oil, such as that made by Basil and Helen Koutalianos of Basil Olive Oil Products in Pitt Meadows, B.C., and a good-quality tomato make a delicious, simple salad. Balance a fruity olive oil with a tomato with good acidity and you don't even need a vinaigrette.

We use Stoney Paradise heirloom tomatoes, which are my favorite here in British Columbia. Any heirloom tomato from a grower in your area is ideal. I like to use Basil and Helen's olive oil not only for its great taste, but also because of my belief in supporting local producers by buying direct from them.

Macerating dried tomatoes in a good-quality olive oil results in a unique-tasting oil to add to sauces, soups, and vinaigrettes. The macerated tomatoes are wonderful for adding taste, texture, and color to winter fare.

SERVES 4 | SERVE WITH RIESLING, MOSEL, GERMANY, KABINETT

TOMATO OIL
6 ripe heirloom tomatoes
Golden Olive Eleni extra
   virgin olive oil or other
   good-quality olive oil

TOMATO SALAD
4 ripe heirloom tomatoes,
   thinly sliced
Pinch of Smoked Sea Salt Flakes
   (see note below)

1 To prepare the tomato oil, preheat the oven to 200°F. Slice, quarter, or halve the tomatoes, depending on their size. Spread the tomatoes out on a wire rack set on a rimmed baking sheet and dry them for 4 to 6 hours or until they are the texture of a plump raisin. The time will vary depending on the juiciness of the tomatoes. (This process may be accelerated by using a food dehydrator.)

2 Put the dried tomatoes in a jar or bowl and add enough olive oil to cover them completely. Macerate for 1 week in the refrigerator to allow the oil to take on an intense tomato flavor. (Freeze the tomatoes in the olive oil for longer storage.)

3 To prepare the tomato salad, arrange a layer of tomato slices on 4 plates and drizzle with the tomato oil. Scatter over a few dried tomatoes for texture and taste. Finish by sprinkling the tomatoes with smoked sea salt flakes.

NOTE   *At C Restaurant we smoke our own salt and it can be ordered online at www .crestaurant.com. It is also available at specialty food stores across Canada. In Vancouver, look for it at The Gourmet Warehouse, Edible British Columbia on Granville Island, and Stongs Market.*

COCONUT SHRIMP
green mango salad | coconut chips

PANDALOPSIS DISPAR

Having only ever been exposed to farmed tiger prawns, I believed I didn't even like shrimp until I moved west and tasted wild B.C. sidestripes. Sweet, succulent, and easy to cook, they are a good alternative to the economically and environmentally devastating southeast Asian farmed product.

If you prefer not to make the coconut chip garnish, substitute 2 table-spoons toasted shredded coconut.

SERVES 4 | SERVE WITH GEWÜRZTRAMINER, ALSACE

COCONUT SHRIMP
1 shallot, sliced
1 clove garlic, minced
1 teaspoon kosher salt
1 teaspoon finely chopped lemongrass
1 teaspoon grated kaffir lime zest
1 cup canned coconut cream
1 pound sidestripe shrimp, peeled and deveined

GREEN MANGO SALAD
1 small green mango, peeled, pitted, and julienned

2 red chilies, chopped
1 tablespoon sliced shallot
1 tablespoon coarsely chopped cilantro
1 tablespoon coarsely chopped mint
1 tablespoon palm sugar
1 tablespoon fish sauce
1 tablespoon freshly squeezed lime juice
Kosher salt

COCONUT CHIPS
1 small coconut

1 To prepare the coconut shrimp, grind the shallot, garlic, salt, lemongrass, and lime zest to a paste using a mortar and pestle or the flat side of a chef's knife. Reduce ½ cup of the coconut cream in a saucepan over medium-high heat, until it separates and starts to darken. Add the paste to the coconut cream and sweat for 30 seconds. Stir in the remaining coconut cream and bring to a boil. Add the shrimp and remove from the heat, allowing the sauce's residual heat to finish the cooking process. Set aside to cool.

2 To prepare the green mango salad, combine all the ingredients in a bowl. Let stand for 30 minutes to allow the flavors to blend.

3 To prepare the coconut chips, preheat the oven to 250°F. Using a hammer or a mallet, break open the outer hard shell of the coconut. Pry out large pieces of the coconut meat from the shell. Using a mandoline slicer, shave the coconut meat into thin, crescent-shaped slices. Spread the slices on a parchment-paper-lined baking sheet or a silicone mat. Bake for about 1 hour or until crunchy and colorless.

4 To serve, create a small mound of the green mango salad on 4 plates and place a few coconut shrimp with a little of their sauce on top. Garnish with the coconut chips.

GRILLED "FARMED ON LAND" PINTO ABALONE

seaweed salad | marinated jellyfish | tobiko

The wild pinto abalone is listed as a threatened species under Canada's Species at Risk Act (SARA), and C Restaurant would like to encourage everyone to help protect this valuable marine creature from further destruction caused by illegal poaching.

The abalone featured in the photograph was legally purchased, under special permit, from the Bamfield Huu ay aht First Nation Community Abalone Project (BHCAP) in Bamfield, B.C. The recipe has been included in this book not to encourage the consumption of abalone, but to highlight one of the many challenges facing our oceans. In conjunction with the Department of Fisheries and Oceans and part of the Bamfield Marine Sciences Centre, BHCAP was created to help rehabilitate the local stocks of wild pinto abalone.

BHCAP's farmed abalone is served exclusively at C Restaurant, and by purchasing this legal abalone we are helping to finance an initiative that will encourage understanding and support for life in our oceans. More information about BHCAP's rehabilitation efforts can be found at www.bms.bc.ca.

SERVES 6 | SERVE WITH VOUVRAY, SEC

6 abalone, shucked

12 ounces prepared wakame salad (seaweed salad found in Japanese stores)

6 ounces prepared shredded jellyfish (found in Asian stores)

1 tablespoon sesame oil

Tobiko (flying fish roe) and soy sauce for garnish

1 Using a spoon or a small flexible plastic putty knife, remove each abalone from its shell. Discard the intestines and, starting from the back of the abalone (the part that was attached to the shell) and working toward the foot (the yellow part that's uppermost when the abalone is still in its shell), slice the meat into thin slivers. When you reach the thicker part of the abalone, stop and reserve this larger piece for grilling.

2 In a bowl, mix the slivers of abalone with the seaweed salad and jellyfish. Set aside.

3 Brush the reserved pieces of abalone with sesame oil. Grill over high heat on a barbecue or in a ridged grill pan just long enough to achieve grill marks and warm the abalone through, a couple of seconds on each side.

4 To serve, thinly slice the grilled abalone on a 45-degree angle. Fan the slices attractively onto 6 plates and garnish with the salad and tobiko. Drizzle with a little additional sesame seed oil and a little soy sauce.

Dungeness crab is abundant from Alaska to California, with some of the best harvested off the Queen Charlotte Islands, here in British Columbia. I love crab—the crustaceans are available year round, and there is nothing better than boiling up a bunch and spending the evening picking the succulent flesh from the shells and chatting with good friends.

Winter melons have green skin and white porous flesh; look for them in Asian produce stores.

SERVES 6 | SERVE WITH VIOGNIER, SOUTH FRANCE

DUNGENESS CRAB

One 2-pound Dungeness crab or 8 ounces cooked Dungeness crab meat

WINTER MELON SALAD

2 tablespoons sliced shallots
1 tablespoon canola oil
2 quarter-size slices fresh ginger
1 teaspoon seeded and chopped Thai red chili
1 cup peeled, seeded, and diced winter melon
3 tablespoons Mayonnaise (see page 140)
2 tablespoons white wine
1 tablespoon chopped cilantro
1 tablespoon sliced green onion
1 tablespoon juice from Preserved Lemons (see page 152) or 1 teaspoon freshly squeezed lemon juice

GARNISH

1 bunch baby arugula, washed and dried
½ cup toasted almonds
¼ cup sliced Preserved Lemons (see page 152)

1 If you choose to cook your own crab, the most humane way to dispatch it is to flip it onto its back and lift up the small arrow-shaped flap in the center toward the back of the shell. Here, you will see a small hole in the shell. Pierce this hole with a sharp screwdriver until you feel it hit the other side of the shell. Flip the crab right side up and let it drain.

2 Immerse the crab in a large pot of boiling salted water and cook for 7 to 10 minutes, depending on the size of the crab. You will see the color change to a brighter hue of pink. Remove the crab from the pot and let it cool.

3 Twist off the crab's legs and claws and set aside. To remove the meat from the body, hold the crab upside down and use your thumbs to push the body up and out of the shell. Discard the stomach sac situated just behind the crab's mouth. Pull away the soft gills attached along the edges and discard them. Cut the body into quarters and remove the meat with a skewer. Open the claws and legs with scissors and remove the meat.

4 To prepare the winter melon salad, sweat the shallots, oil, ginger, and chili in a heavy bottomed saucepan over medium heat for 2 minutes. Add the winter melon and cook for 3 to 4 minutes. Deglaze with the white wine, then reduce until the mixture is almost dry. Remove the ginger slices and discard. Set the mixture aside to cool.

5 To serve, stir the crab meat into the melon mixture, along with the mayonnaise, cilantro, green onion, and preserved lemon juice. Divide the arugula among 6 plates. Place a mound of crab salad on each bed of arugula. Garnish each plate with toasted almonds and a small slice of preserved lemon.

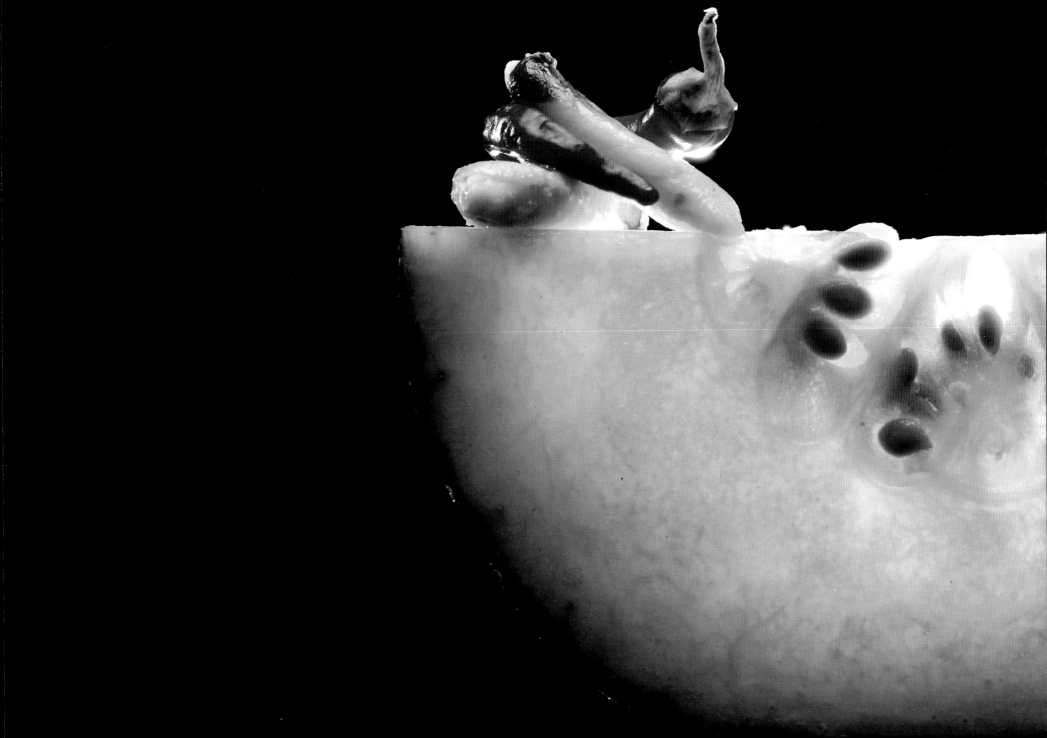

TOMATO CONSOMMÉ

cherrystone clams | multicolored chard | Oyama chorizo

MERCENARIA MERCENARIA

Cured meats and shellfish are combined in cuisines all over the world, and there is no place where the marriage works better than here in Vancouver. With the exceptional artisan-cured meat products from Oyama Sausage Company, and our access to great local clams, it's only natural that we team them at C Restaurant.

SERVES 10 | SERVE WITH POUILLY-FUMÉ

TOMATO FENNEL CONSOMMÉ

Three 28-ounce cans whole
    plum tomatoes, chopped
1 cup diced onion
8 egg whites
1 cup water
½ cup diced fennel
¼ cup diced celery
2 cups lightly packed basil leaves
4 cloves garlic, cut in half
1 teaspoon granulated sugar
1 teaspoon kosher salt
½ teaspoon black pepper
½ teaspoon saffron threads
¼ teaspoon grated nutmeg

GARNISH

5 ounces chorizo, julienned
10 raw cherrystone clams,
    shucked
1 cup assorted-colored chard
    stalks, julienned

1 To prepare the tomato consommé, stir together all the ingredients in a large heavy bottomed stock pot, ensuring the even distribution of egg whites. Bring to a simmer, stirring constantly with a wooden spoon or rubber spatula to prevent the egg whites from sticking to the bottom of the pot. When white foam begins to form around the edge of the pot, stop stirring, reduce the heat to low, and simmer, uncovered, for 2 to 3 hours. The egg whites will rise to form a "raft," bringing all the impurities to the surface, and leaving a clear, intensely flavored liquid below. Strain the consommé through 3 layers of cheesecloth or a fine-mesh strainer. Allow the solids to drip for an hour or so to increase the yield.

2 Sauté the chorizo in a small skillet over medium-high heat until golden. Drain on paper towels.

3 To serve, reheat the consommé until steaming. Divide the chorizo, raw clams, and chard stalks among 10 shallow bowls. Ladle the steaming tomato consommé over the top.

CHILLED FENNEL CONSOMMÉ
fresh mussels | fried basil

British Columbia produces some of the best mussels in the world, and I love to serve them with fennel and tomato in as many ways as possible. Here we have had a bit of fun and created a jellied consommé, but the recipe is also great without the addition of gelatin. Simply ladle the consommé over the mussels and serve chilled in the height of summer, or hot during the cold, wet months of winter.

SERVES 8 | SERVE WITH GRÜNER VELTLINER, AUSTRIA

JELLIED MUSSELS

4 cups of Tomato Fennel
    Consommé (see recipe page 18)
8 sheets gelatin or 2 tablespoons
    unflavored powdered gelatin
1 pound mussels, cooked and
    shelled
1 tablespoon coarsely chopped
    dill or fennel tops

GARNISH

Vegetable oil for deep-frying
Basil leaves, washed and dried

1 To prepare the jellied mussels, reheat the 4 cups of reserved consommé until steaming. Put ¼ cup of the hot consommé in the top of a double boiler. Temper the gelatin sheets by placing them in a bowl of cold water for 2 minutes to soften. Squeeze out the excess water. Stir the soaked gelatin into the consommé in the double boiler until completely melted. Stir the gelatin mixture into the remaining hot fennel consommé. If using powdered gelatin, put 2 tablespoons cold water in a small bowl and sprinkle gelatin over the surface. Let stand for 5 minutes or until puffy. Put the bowl in a small saucepan containing enough barely simmering water to come halfway up the sides of the bowl. Stir for 1 minute or until the gelatin is completely melted. Whisk the gelatin into the consommé in the double boiler. Let cool but do not allow to set.

2 Divide the mussels evenly among eight ¾-cup molds. Sprinkle evenly with chopped dill or fennel tops. Pour the cooled fennel consommé evenly into the molds. Refrigerate for at least 2 hours or until set.

3 Pour the oil into a deep fryer and heat to 375°F following the manufacturer's instructions. Deep-fry the basil leaves for a few seconds or until crisp. Drain the basil leaves on paper towel.

4 To serve, run warm water over the bases of the molds to loosen the jellies. Invert each onto a plate. Garnish with the fried basil leaves.

Bottarga is the salted, pressed, and dried roe of tuna or gray mullet (traditionally known as "poor man's caviar"). All year long, we receive Kagan Bay scallops, and during some months their roe gets wonderfully large and plump. Not wishing to waste it, we smoke it and make it into scallop bottarga. Instead, you can substitute real bottarga, which is available from Italian supermarkets or online.

Using a pressure cooker to prepare the pea consommé creates a crystal-clear liquid that adds a very intense pea flavor to the soup.

SERVES 4 | SERVE WITH RIESLING, NEW WORLD

PEA CONSOMMÉ

4 pounds fresh green peas
   in their pods
½ cup water

PEA SOUP

Shelled peas reserved
   from consommé
½ cup sliced shallots
6 tablespoons cold unsalted
   butter
Kosher salt, black pepper,
   and grated nutmeg

GARNISH

Grated bottarga

1 To prepare the pea consommé, shell the peas, setting the peas aside and reserving the pods. Combine the pea pods and water in a pressure cooker and cook at high pressure, following the manufacturer's instructions, for 3 to 4 minutes or until the pods are very tender. Set aside to steep in the pressure cooker for 30 minutes. Strain the consommé through 3 layers of cheesecloth or a fine-mesh strainer.

2 To prepare the pea soup, blanch the shelled peas in boiling salted water for about 15 seconds, then immediately refresh in ice water. Drain well and set aside. In a heavy bottomed saucepan, sweat the shallots with 3 tablespoons of the butter until they are soft and translucent. Add the pea consommé and bring to a boil. Season with salt, pepper, and nutmeg to taste. Add the blanched peas and return the soup to a simmer. Remove from the heat and purée in a blender (not a food processor) until smooth. To retain the soup's bright green color, cool it down

3 To serve, reheat the soup over medium heat until steaming. Remove from the heat and whisk in the remaining butter. Ladle into 4 shallow bowls. Garnish with grated bottarga.

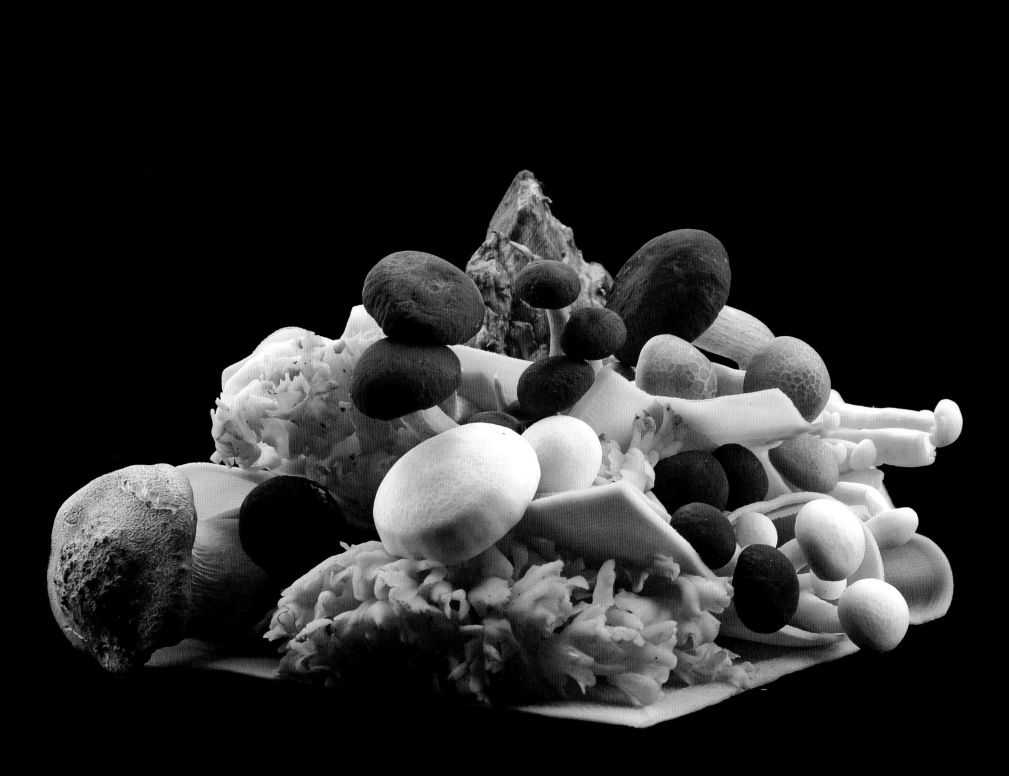

BRAISED MUSHROOMS WITH DRIED TOFU

green onions | iron buddha black bean sauce

As blessed as British Columbia is with seafood, our variety of wild and cultivated mushrooms are also deserving of attention. This shot is one of my favorites and always makes me want to get into the kitchen and cook something with mushrooms. Dried tofu is sometimes hard to find but any tofu works well with the sauce.

To make ginger juice, grate fresh ginger into a fine-mesh strainer and press on it firmly to extract the juice; discard the ginger pulp.

SERVES 4 | SERVE WITH SAKE, YAMAHAI

BRAISED MUSHROOMS
1 teaspoon peanut oil
9 ounces assorted mushrooms, such as chanterelle, shiitake, oyster, golden foot, or pine, cleaned and trimmed

IRON BUDDHA BLACK BEAN SAUCE
⅔ cup boiling water
3 tablespoons Iron Buddha tea leaves
2 tablespoons fermented black beans, soaked overnight

1 teaspoon your favorite chili paste
1 clove garlic, minced
2 tablespoons peanut oil
1 shallot, sliced
4 teaspoons ginger juice
4 teaspoons black rice vinegar
2 ounces dried tofu, drained, patted very dry, and cut into pastalike strips
2 tablespoons sweet soy sauce
1 tablespoon light soy sauce
Sliced green onions for garnish

1 To prepare the braised mushrooms, heat a wide shallow sauté pan over medium-high heat. Add the oil, then quickly sauté the mushrooms until they are golden brown and tender. Remove the mushrooms from the pan and set aside. Do not wash the pan.

2 To prepare the Iron Buddha black bean sauce, pour the boiling water over the tea leaves. Let the tea brew for 10 minutes, then strain, discarding the leaves. In a bowl, crush the soaked black beans with the back of a fork and mix in the chili paste and garlic.

3 Heat the sauté pan over medium heat. Add the oil and sauté the shallots and black bean mixture, until the shallot is soft and translucent. Deglaze the pan with the tea, ginger juice, and black rice vinegar. Add the tofu and sweet and light soy sauces. Simmer for 2 minutes or until the mixture begins to achieve a sauce-like consistency. Add the cooked mushrooms and toss well. Divide the mushroom mixture among 4 plates. Garnish with the sliced green onions.

FISH & SEAFOOD

BAYNE SOUND SCALLOP
coriander-grapefruit jelly | grapefruit segments

PATINOPECTEN CAURINUS (HYBRID WEATHERVANE SCALLOP) | PATINOPECTEN YESSOENSIS (JAPANESE SCALLOP)

There is nothing better than a fresh scallop, and here in British Columbia we are blessed with wonderfully tasting and sustainably produced varieties, such as the shellfish from Island Scallops in Qualicum Beach. Frozen scallops are often pumped with water (that you end up paying for because of the weight it adds). Regardless of what you may be told, if you see scallops in a display case sitting in liquid, you can guarantee they have been previously frozen.

Agar-agar powder is a flavorless setting agent made from dried seaweed; look for it in specialty food stores and Asian grocery stores.

SERVES 8 | SERVE WITH SAUVIGNON BLANC, NEW WORLD

CORIANDER-GRAPEFRUIT JELLY
1 cup freshly squeezed grapefruit juice
1 cup apple juice
2 teaspoons coriander seeds, toasted and crushed
¼ teaspoon orange blossom water (found in Middle Eastern stores)
2 tablespoons water
1 teaspoon agar-agar powder

GARNISH
8 raw Bayne Sound scallops, cut into paper-thin slices
Grapefruit segments for garnish

1 To prepare the coriander-grapefruit jelly, bring the grapefruit juice, apple juice, coriander seeds, and orange blossom water to a simmer in a nonreactive saucepan. Remove the saucepan from the heat and let stand for 1 hour to allow the flavors to infuse. Strain the juice and return to the saucepan. Bring to a boil. Whisk together the water and agar-agar powder until the powder dissolves. Whisk this mixture into the juice and simmer for 1 minute. Pour the juice into eight ½-cup molds. Refrigerate for at least 2 hours or until set.

2 To serve, run warm water over bases of the molds to loosen the jellies. Invert each onto a plate. Garnish with the raw scallops and grapefruit segments.

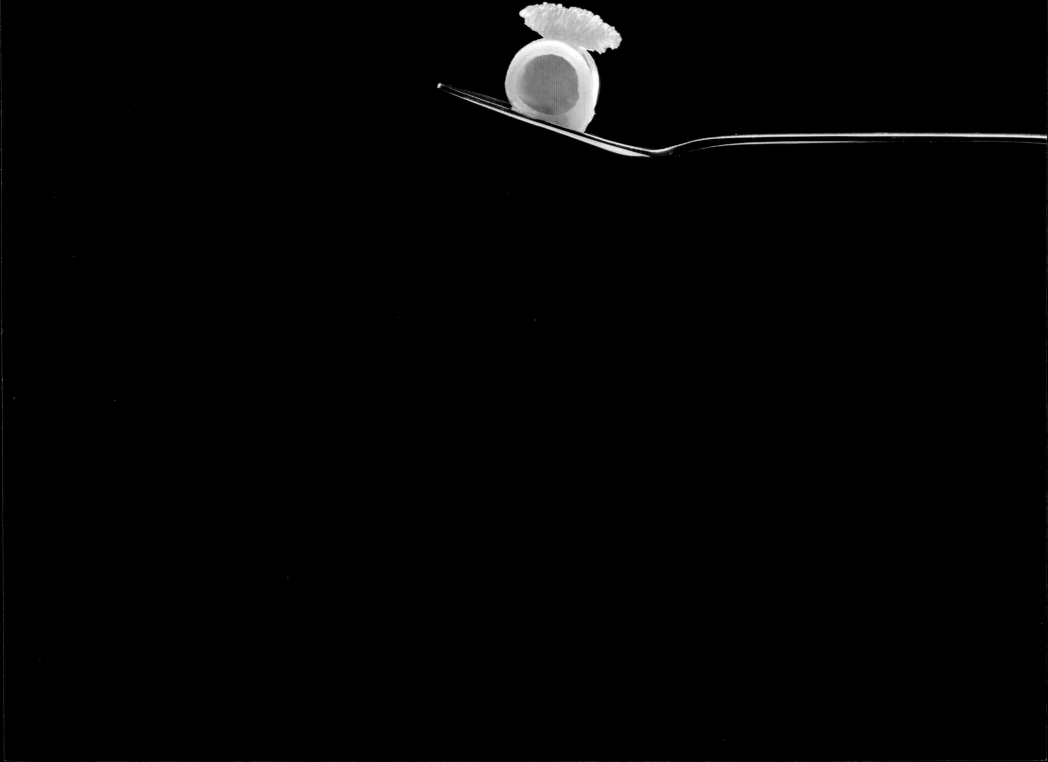

I'm always amused at the number of people who'll happily enjoy a plate of fried calamari along with their pitcher of beer, all the while claiming they'd never eat squid even for a bet.

SERVES 4 | SERVE WITH PROSECCO

SQUID

1 pound cleaned squid bodies
2 cups buttermilk
2 teaspoons kosher salt
1 cup flour seasoned with kosher
  salt and black pepper
Vegetable oil for deep-frying

CRÈME FRAÎCHE–HABANERO DIP

1 tablespoon chopped cilantro
½ habanero pepper, seeded
  and finely diced
1 cup Crème Fraîche
  (see page 112)

BEER BATTER

1 cup potato starch
1 cup all-purpose flour
¼ cup Seven C's Spice Blend
  (see page 130)
2 teaspoons baking powder
1½ cups lager, ale, or dark beer

GARNISH

Kosher salt
1 lime, cut into wedges

1 To prepare the squid, cut the squid bodies crosswise into ¼-inch slices. Stir together the buttermilk and salt in a nonreactive bowl. Add the squid and refrigerate for 2 hours.

2 Drain the squid, discarding the buttermilk. Dredge the squid in seasoned flour to coat completely. Gently lay the squid on a baking sheet and set aside for 10 minutes to allow the squid to dry and firm up slightly. Pour the oil into a deep fryer and heat to 350°F following the manufacturer's instructions.

3 To prepare the crème fraîche–habanero dip, fold the cilantro and habanero pepper into the crème fraîche and set aside.

4 To prepare the beer batter, whisk together the potato starch, flour, spice blend, and baking powder. Pour in the lager and stir until smooth.

5 Dip the squid rings one at a time in the beer batter and deep-fry, a few at a time, for 2 to 3 minutes or until crisp and golden brown. Drain the squid on paper towel and season with salt to taste.

6 To serve, place the squid in a napkin-lined bread basket or bowl, and squeeze the lime juice over the top. Serve with the crème fraîche–habanero dip.

BRITISH COLUMBIAN GEODUCK
horseradish cream | roasted beet | parsley purée

PANOPEA ABRUPTA

My favorite clam, geoduck (pronounced "gooey-duck"), is great raw, simply marinated in a dash of soy sauce or a touch of ponzu, or folded into this horseradish-spiked sauce and served as a canapé. To appreciate geoduck's unique qualities, it's very important not to overcook it. The easiest way to avoid this is to make the sauce, bring it to a boil, then stir in the clam meat and immediately remove the saucepan from the heat. The residual heat will be enough to cook the geoduck perfectly.

Geoduck must be very fresh. Buy it only a few hours before you serve it and have your fishmonger slice it for you.

MAKES ABOUT 20 CANAPÉS | SERVE WITH MANZANILLA FINO SHERRY

ROASTED BEETS

2 pounds baby beets, trimmed
Kosher salt and black pepper
½ cup unsalted butter

PARSLEY PURÉE

2 cups flat-leaf parsley leaves
   (no stems)
1 tablespoon vegetable stock

GEODUCK IN HORSERADISH CREAM

3 shallots, sliced
1 tablespoon unsalted butter
½ cup white wine
2 teaspoons tarragon vinegar
1 cup whipping cream (35%)
2 teaspoons creamed horseradish
1 pound fresh geoduck, sliced
Kosher salt

1 To prepare the roasted beets, preheat the oven to 375°F. Scrub the beets, leaving their skins on. Put the beets on a sheet of aluminum foil large enough to enclose them completely. Season with salt and pepper to taste, and dot with the butter. Wrap the beets in the foil, sealing the edges well. Roast for 1 hour or until tender.

2 To prepare the parsley purée, blanch the parsley leaves in boiling salted water for about 5 seconds, then immediately refresh in ice water. Drain the leaves, then purée them with the stock in a blender (not a food processor) until smooth. Avoid leaving the purée in the blender for too long as the heat from the motor will cause it to darken to an unattractive color.

3 To prepare the horseradish cream, sweat the shallots in the butter in a saucepan over medium-low heat until they are soft and translucent. Deglaze with the wine and vinegar, then simmer until the liquid is reduced by two-thirds. Add the cream. Reduce again by one-third, then stir in the creamed horseradish. Fold in the geoduck and remove the saucepan from the heat. Season with salt to taste.

4 To serve, thinly slice the baby beets and place each slice on a spoon. Top each beet slice with a dollop of creamed geoduck. Drizzle the parsley purée over the top or to the side of each canapé.

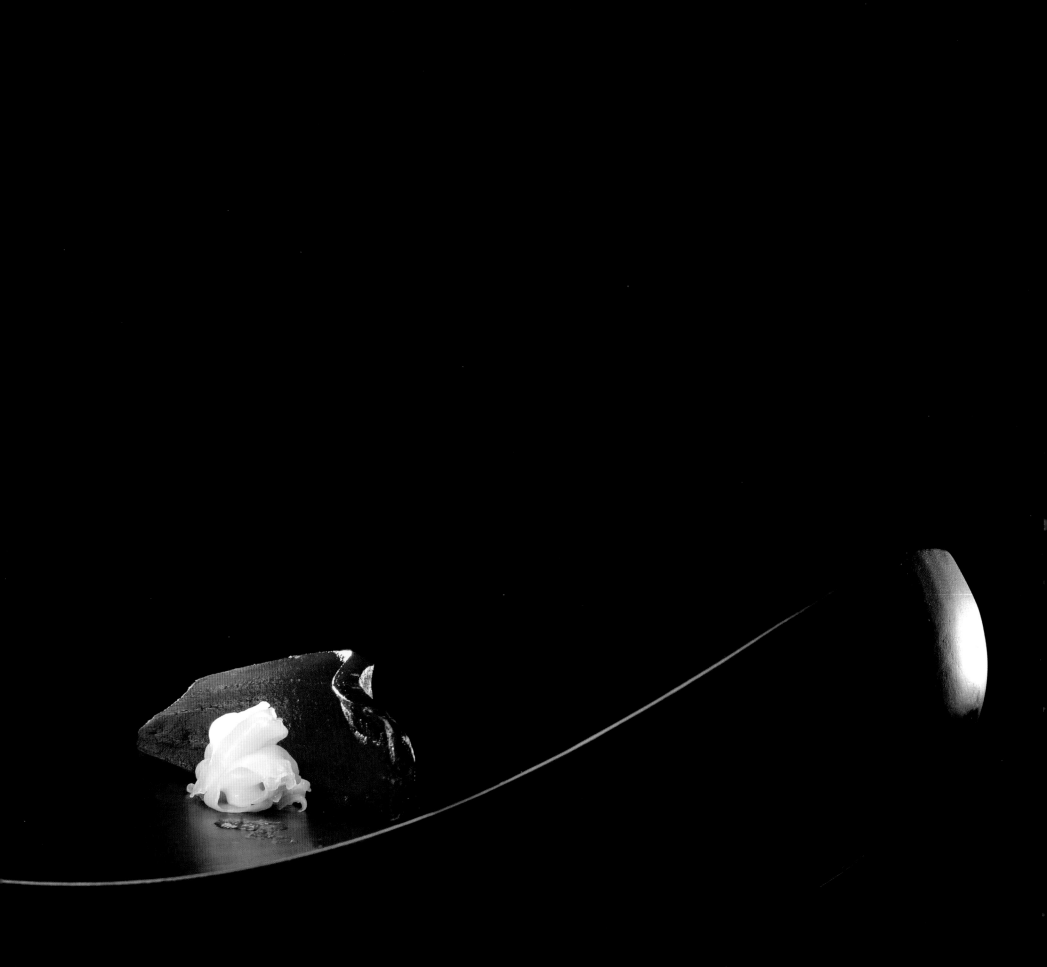

The lowly octopus was, in the early years of C Restaurant, the inspiration behind many of our creations. Historically shunned by North Americans, its ability to be brined, braised, smoked, or grilled demonstrated to us its versatility and led us to create our now signature ingredient—house-made "octopus bacon."

SERVES 8 | SERVE WITH CHABLIS

OCTOPUS

2 cups water

⅓ cup kosher salt

2 tablespoons granulated sugar

2 pounds octopus

BRAISE

4 cups water

1 onion, coarsely chopped

1 whole head of garlic,
   cut in half

3 tablespoons kosher salt

1 tablespoon black peppercorns

1 small bunch thyme

4 bay leaves

EGGPLANT PURÉE

1 large eggplant

2 tablespoons kosher salt

1 lemon, zested and juiced

2 tablespoons extra virgin
   olive oil

1 clove garlic, crushed

Kosher salt and black pepper

GARNISH

Extra virgin olive oil

Freshly squeezed lemon juice

Preserved Lemons (see
   page 152), sliced

1 To prepare the octopus, stir together the water, salt, and sugar in a narrow nonreactive container. Add the octopus, ensuring it is completely submerged (if it isn't, use a narrower container). Refrigerated for 4 hours to cure the octopus.

2 To prepare the braise, remove the octopus from the brine and place in a heavy bottomed saucepan. Add the braising ingredients. Braise the octopus by simmering it gently for 3½ hours or until tender. Remove the saucepan from the heat and allow the octopus to cool in the liquid until it is cool enough to handle. Remove the octopus from the saucepan, discarding the water and aromatics. Drain the octopus well.

3 To prepare the eggplant purée, cut the eggplant in half lengthwise and score the flesh in a diamond pattern, being careful not to cut the skin. Rub the salt into the flesh of each half and let stand for 30 minutes. (This draws out the bitter liquid in the eggplant.) Preheat the oven to 350°F. Rinse the salt off the eggplant and squeeze each half to remove any excess liquid. Place the eggplant, flesh side down, on a baking sheet and roast for about 20 minutes or until the skin is charred and the flesh is soft. When cool enough to handle, scoop the flesh from each eggplant half. Purée the eggplant flesh, lemon zest and juice, olive oil, and garlic in a food processor (not a blender) until smooth. Season with salt and pepper to taste.

4 Brush the octopus lightly with olive oil and grill over high heat on the barbecue or in a ridged grill pan, just long enough to achieve grill marks and warm the octopus through, a couple of minutes on each side. Cut the octopus into bite-size pieces and drizzle with lemon juice.

5 To serve, create a small mound of eggplant purée on each of 8 plates and stack the octopus pieces on top. Garnish with sliced preserved lemons.

PACIFIC OYSTERS

mignonette fizz | cracker straw

CRASSOSTREA GIGAS

Sweet, plump, and as refreshing as a sea breeze, farmed Pacific oysters are usually available most of the year. Marketed under a variety of names, they are grown in different regions of the province from the same seed stock, but take on unique taste profiles depending on the water that they are raised in.

If you have a kitchen scale, weigh out the ingredients for the Armenian Cracker Straws for best results.

SERVES 4 | SERVE WITH MUSCADET

RED WINE VINEGAR POWDER
6 cups red wine vinegar

2 tablespoons cornstarch

SHALLOT POWDER
8 shallots, thinly sliced

MIGNONETTE FIZZ
1 cup red wine vinegar powder

1 tablespoon shallot powder

2 teaspoons ground bay leaves

2 teaspoons icing sugar

2 teaspoons baking soda

1 teaspoon black pepper

1 teaspoon kosher salt

1 teaspoon citric acid

ARMENIAN CRACKER STRAWS
6⅔ cups (1 kilogram) all-purpose flour

1½ tablespoons (20 grams) kosher salt

1½ tablespoons (20 grams) granulated sugar

Pinch of dry yeast

1¾ cups warm water

3 eggs

½ cup (125 grams) unsalted butter, melted

Dash of freshly squeezed lemon juice

24 wooden chopsticks

OYSTERS
Kosher salt

48 Pacific oysters

CONTINUED ON PAGE 41 . . .

PACIFIC OYSTERS *(continued)*

1 To prepare the red wine vinegar powder, simmer the vinegar in a nonreactive saucepan until it is reduced by half. Pour 1 tablespoon of the reduced red wine vinegar into a bowl and add the cornstarch. Stir until smooth. Whisk the cornstarch mixture into the simmering vinegar and boil for 1 minute, stirring constantly. Pour the reduced vinegar onto a parchment-paper-lined baking sheet and allow to dry at room temperature until very brittle. This will take several days. Grind to a fine powder in a spice grinder.

2 To prepare the shallot powder, preheat the oven to 200°F. Spread the shallot slices on a baking sheet and bake for several hours, until crisp and dry. (This process may be accelerated by using a food dehydrator.) Grind to a fine powder in a spice grinder.

3 To prepare the mignonette fizz, combine all the ingredients and pass through a fine-mesh sieve. Store in an airtight container until needed.

4 To prepare the Armenian Cracker Straws, preheat the oven to 400°F. Whisk together the flour and salt in a large bowl. In a separate large bowl, dissolve the sugar and yeast in the warm water and let stand for 5 minutes. Beat together the eggs, melted butter, and lemon juice in a separate bowl, then beat into the yeast mixture. Add the flour mixture and knead for 10 minutes to form a firm dough. Let the dough rest at room temperature for 30 minutes.

5 Divide the dough into 24 pieces. Roll out 1 piece of pastry to a thin sheet on a lightly floured surface. Roll the sheet of dough around a chopstick to form a straw. Repeat with remaining dough and chopsticks. Put the straws, with the chopsticks, on a baking sheet and bake for 7 to 10 minutes or until crisp and golden. While still warm, remove the chopsticks and allow the straws to cool on a wire rack. Store the cracker straws in an airtight container.

6 To prepare the oysters, spread a layer of salt on 4 plates. Shuck the oysters and arrange oysters in their shells on the salt. Place 1 teaspoon of mignonette fizz on each oyster. The liquid in the oyster will react with the baking soda and vinegar powder and begin to fizz. Serve with the Armenian Cracker Straws.

STEAMED ALASKAN KING CRAB LEGS

candied orange butter | organic mixed greens

PARALITHODES CAMTSCHATICUS

Alaskan king crabs are the most unbelievably delicious tasting in the world. They're unbeatable when purchased fresh and cooked alive; frozen Alaskan crab legs pale in comparison. Although I'm a vocal advocate of frozen quality seafood, in this case I would encourage you to buy only fresh king crab. Alaskan king crab is considered OK, but not great, in terms of sustainability, so we don't cook it in the restaurant unless it's specially requested. Nor is there usually any need since we have access to a local, more sustainable option—Dungeness crab—which, of course, goes equally well with our candied orange butter!

SERVES 4 | SERVE WITH VIOGNIER, CALIFORNIA

CRAB

1 small live king crab
2 tablespoons unsalted butter
½ cup sliced shallots
1 clove garlic, sliced
2 bay leaves
6 black peppercorns
1 cup water
½ cup white wine
½ cup freshly squeezed
   orange juice

CANDIED ORANGE BUTTER

½ cup hot reduced crab
   cooking liquid
½ cup cold unsalted butter, cubed
2 tablespoons chopped candied
   orange
1 teaspoon freshly squeezed
   lemon juice
Pinch of kosher salt

SALAD

1 bunch organic mixed
   greens (optional)

1 To prepare the crab, melt the butter over medium heat in a heavy bottomed pot large enough to hold the crab. Sweat the shallots, garlic, bay leaves, and peppercorns for 3 minutes or until the shallots are soft and translucent. Increase the heat to high and add the water, white wine, and orange juice. When the liquid begins to boil, add the crab, cover and cook for 7 to 10 minutes, depending on the size of the crab. You will see the color change to a dark red hue. Remove the crab from the pot and let it cool. Strain the cooking liquid into a smaller saucepan. Simmer until it is reduced to ½ cup. (This will add intense flavor to the candied orange butter.)

2 When the crab is cool enough to handle, detach the top of its shell from the rest of the body. Discard the stomach sac situated just behind the crab's mouth. Pull away the soft gills attached along the edges and discard them. Cut the body down the middle and twist off each leg. Crack the legs at the knuckles, separating each at the joints. Use sturdy kitchen scissors to cut the crab in half lengthwise to expose the meat. Either remove the meat from the legs and body or leave intact for a more casual meal.

3 To prepare the candied orange butter, place the hot reduced cooking liquid in a blender (not a food processor). With the motor on medium speed, gradually add the cold cubed butter 1 piece at a time. Still with the motor running, add the chopped candied orange and lemon juice, and blend until the mixture is fairly smooth. Season with salt to taste.

4 To serve, either toss the crab meat with the warm candied orange butter and serve over a bed of organic greens, or leave the meat intact and serve the crab in its shell with the candied orange butter for dipping.

LOBSTER SASHIMI
miso soup | tobiko

This was a favorite dish on C Restaurant's menu in the late '90s, and we would often accompany it with an ounce of cognac to serve as a dipping sauce for the slivers of raw lobster.

Lobsters should always be alive prior to cooking. When buying lobster from the market or fishmonger, choose a lively one with a tail that springs back when straightened. Its shell should be thick and hard as this usually indicates good-quality meat.

SERVES 4 | SERVE WITH CHAMPAGNE, BLANC DE BLANCS

LOBSTER
1 live lobster (about 2 pounds)

MISO SOUP
4 cups water
One 3-inch piece kombu
   (Japanese seaweed)
1 ounce bonito flakes
¼ cup mirin

¼ cup Japanese soy sauce
1 tablespoon granulated sugar
1 tablespoon white, yellow,
   or red miso

GARNISH
1 teaspoon tobiko (flying fish roe)
1 green onion, thinly sliced
   diagonally

1 To prepare the lobster, hold it firmly on a cutting board and plunge the tip of a sharp chef's knife right through the lobster's head, just behind its eyes. Cut the lobster tail from its body. Using sturdy kitchen scissors, cut out the underbelly from the tail and remove the raw lobster meat in 1 piece, using a spoon or a clam knife to separate the flesh from the top of the shell. Slice the lobster tail crosswise into thin slices.

2 Remove the lobster claws and legs from its head. Cook them in boiling salted water for about 3 minutes, then drain well. When cool enough to handle, crack the claws and legs and remove the meat from the shells. Set aside.

3 To prepare the miso soup, combine the water and kombu in a nonreactive bowl and let soak in the refrigerator overnight. The following day, pour the water and seaweed into a nonreactive saucepan and bring to a simmer. Remove the saucepan from the heat, add the bonito flakes and steep for 10 to 15 minutes.

4 Strain the stock through 3 layers of cheesecloth or a fine-mesh strainer. Return to the saucepan and stir in the mirin, soy, and sugar. Bring the soup back to a simmer for 2 minutes, then remove the saucepan from the heat. Stir in the miso.

5 To serve, fan the lobster sashimi on 4 plates and sprinkle with the tobiko. Ladle the miso soup into 4 soup bowls and garnish with the reserved cooked lobster meat and green onion.

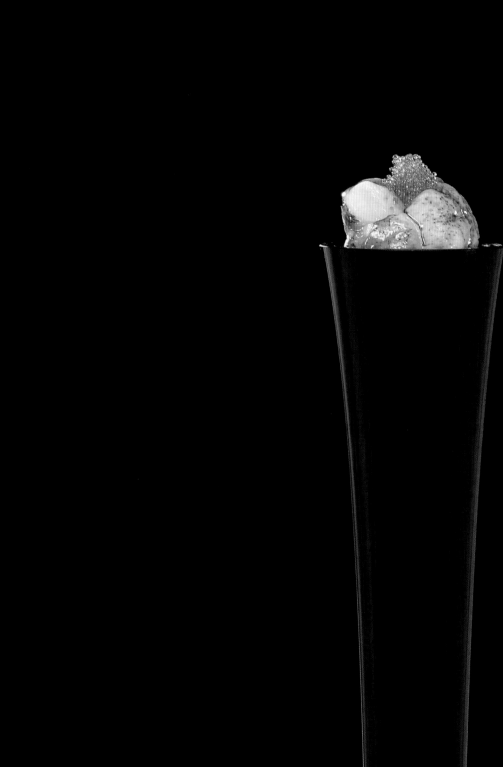

Although C Restaurant built its reputation by serving local, high-quality, and sustainably caught British Columbian seafood, we have always thought that to be a leading Canadian seafood restaurant, we needed to have Nova Scotia lobster on the menu. Recognizable and popular, the lobster sat quietly at the bottom of our menu, never being highlighted or promoted, but rather serving as a comforting and familiar option while we faced the challenges of reintroducing new or overlooked seafood choices that were local and sustainable.

SERVES 4 | SERVE WITH WHITE BURGUNDY

LOBSTER

2 gallons water

1 cup kosher salt

1 pound asparagus

2 live lobsters (each 1½ pounds)

MOREL SAUCE

8 ounces fresh morels

2 tablespoons sliced shallot

2 tablespoons unsalted butter

½ cup white wine

½ cup Veal Jus (see page 134)

1 tablespoon chopped thyme leaves

Kosher salt and black pepper

1 To prepare the lobster, bring the water and salt to a boil in a large pot. Blanch the asparagus for 30 seconds then, reserving the blanching water, immediately refresh the asparagus in ice water to maintain its vibrant color. Drain and set aside.

2 Bring the salted water back to a rolling boil and add the lobsters. Cook for 5 to 6 minutes. You will see the color change to a dark red hue. Remove the lobsters from the pot and, when cool enough to handle, separate the tail, legs and claws from the body. Use lobster crackers to remove all the meat from the claws and legs. To remove the meat from the tail, use your hands to apply pressure to both sides of the shell until it cracks and pops open.

3 To prepare the morel sauce, sauté the morels and shallot in 1 tablespoon of the butter for 2 minutes until the shallot is soft and translucent. Add the white wine and reduce until the saucepan is almost dry. Add the veal jus and thyme and bring to a boil. Remove the saucepan from the heat and whisk in the remaining butter. Add the asparagus to the sauce and reheat over very low heat.

4 To serve, spoon some of the asparagus and morel sauce on 4 plates and top with the lobster meat. Drizzle any remaining sauce around each plate.

49

B.C. SARDINES WRAPPED IN BACON
spinach | pine nuts | mustard paper

SARDINOPS SAGAX

B.C. sardines are wonderful, delicious, and healthy, and a far cry from the canned variety that most of us are familiar with. Frozen sardines are available all year; start looking for fresh ones in restaurants and fish stores in early May.

SERVES 4 | SERVE WITH MARSANNE, FRANCE

SARDINES
4 whole sardines
2 tablespoons kosher salt
2 tablespoons granulated sugar
1 teaspoon dill seeds, toasted and ground
12 paper-thin slices double-smoked bacon
Bacon fat for frying

SPINACH
1 tablespoon pine nuts
1 tablespoon unsalted butter
2 cups baby spinach
Pinch of kosher salt

GARNISH
French Dressing (see page 131)
4 pieces Mustard Paper (see page 141)

1 To prepare the sardines, clean and fillet them or ask your fishmonger to do this for you. Stir together the salt, sugar, and dill seeds in a bowl. In a shallow glass dish large enough to hold the sardine fillets in a single layer, sprinkle half of the salt mixture in an even layer to cover the bottom completely. Place the sardine fillets, skin side down, on the salt mixture and sprinkle with the remaining mixture over the top. Cover the fish with plastic wrap and place another slightly smaller dish on top. Set an object weighing about 2 pounds on top of this second dish. Allow the fish to cure in the refrigerator for 4 hours.

2 Remove the sardine fillets from the dish and rinse off the salt mixture. Team the sardine fillets together in pairs, skin side out, and putting the head end of one next to the tail end of another. Lay 3 slices of bacon on the counter with their long sides just overlapping. Lay a pair of sardine fillets on one end of the bacon slices, then roll up to enclose fillets completely and form a cylinder. Lay a square of plastic wrap on the counter and place the cylinder in the center of the edge of the cling wrap closest to you. Wrap the cylinder tightly in the plastic wrap by rolling it away from you, twisting the excess plastic wrap at each end in opposite directions to increase the pres-

sure on the cylinder and to firm it up. Repeat with the remaining sardine fillets and bacon to make 4 cylinders in all. Refrigerate the cylinders for at least 3 hours or overnight to set them.

3 Heat an ovenproof skillet over medium heat and add a little bacon fat. Remove the plastic wrap from the cylinders, then fry them, turning often, for 3 to 5 minutes or until the bacon is crisped to your liking, turning the cylinders twice to keep color even on all sides. Remove the cylinders from the skillet and let rest in a warm place.

4 To prepare the spinach, sauté the pine nuts in the butter in a heavy bottomed sauté pan until golden brown. Add the spinach and salt and cook just until the spinach is wilted.

5 To serve, divide the spinach among 4 plates. Cut the sardine cylinders in half crosswise, place on top of the spinach and drizzle with French dressing. Garnish with the mustard paper.

If you can find troll- or pole-caught yellowfin tuna, often marketed under the Hawaiian name "ahi" here in North America, it would be a better choice than the threatened bluefin tuna. At many fish stores or markets, it's hard to really know what you are buying or how it was caught, so ask a lot of questions.

Black truffle carpaccio is cheaper than whole black truffles; look for it in specialty food stores.

TRUFFLE SYRUP

1 cup granulated sugar

¾ cup sherry vinegar

1 ounce black truffle carpaccio, very finely minced

Kosher salt and black pepper

3 tablespoons good-quality black-truffle-infused oil

NASTURTIUM PURÉE

2 cups nasturtium leaves

AHI TUNA

12 ounces finest quality ahi tuna, sliced into thick sashimi-style slices

1 To prepare the truffle syrup, caramelize the sugar in a heavy bottomed saucepan over medium heat until golden and liquid. Standing back in case the mixture splatters, add the sherry vinegar and cook for 5 minutes. Add the black truffle carpaccio, and reduce by half. The mixture should be the consistency of maple syrup; if it's too runny, reduce it further or, if too thick, add a little water. Remove the saucepan from the heat, season the syrup with salt and pepper to taste, and set aside to cool. Stir in the truffle oil.

2 To prepare the nasturtium purée, blanch the nasturtium leaves in boiling salted water for 2 minutes then, reserving the blanching water, immediately refresh in ice water. Drain the leaves and purée in a blender (not a food processor) until smooth, adding a little of the reserved blanching water, if necessary, to achieve a smooth consistency. Avoid leaving the purée in the blender for too long as the heat from the motor will cause it to darken to an unattractive color. Pour into a coffee-filter-lined sieve or fine-mesh strainer and allow to drain overnight in the fridge. Discard the water that drains from the purée.

3 To serve, divide the tuna among 4 plates. Garnish with the truffle syrup and nasturtium purée.

SEARED ALBACORE TUNA
watermelon three ways

THUNNUS ALALUNGA

Canadian wild albacore's quality, consistency, and sustainability ensures its place not only on C Restaurant's menu, but now on most seafood menus in Vancouver. As the skill levels of our young, upcoming chefs rise and they learn to work with this delicate product, albacore in its "frozen fresh" form has come of age in mainstream restaurants.

The watermelon pickle for this recipe can be prepared days or weeks in advance.

SERVES 4 | SERVE WITH ALBARIÑO

WATERMELON PICKLE

2 pounds watermelon rind

5 cups water

3 tablespoons kosher salt

4 cups granulated sugar

2 cups white wine vinegar

One 3-inch piece fresh ginger, peeled and sliced

1 lemon, zested and juiced

WATERMELON EMULSION

2 cups chopped peeled watermelon

¼ cup sesame seeds, toasted

1 tablespoon sesame oil

Black sesame seed salt or shichimi-togarashi (Japanese seasoning)

ALBACORE TUNA

4 pieces (each 4 ounces) albacore tuna

GARNISH

1 cup diced peeled watermelon tossed with a squeeze of lime juice

20 mint leaves

4 Lime Crackers (see page 138)

1 To prepare the watermelon pickle, cut the watermelon rind into ½-inch cubes, leaving a small portion of pink flesh on for color. Soak the rind in the water and salt for 24 hours. Drain, discarding the brine, and place the rind in a heavy bottomed saucepan. Add enough fresh water to cover the rind and simmer for 20 minutes. Drain well.

2 In a heavy bottomed nonreactive saucepan, bring the remaining pickle ingredients to a boil. Reduce the heat and simmer for 15 minutes. Add the drained watermelon rind and cook until the pieces are translucent. Remove the saucepan from the heat and allow the rind to cool in the liquid. Refrigerate until needed.

3 To prepare the watermelon emulsion, purée the watermelon, sesame seeds, and sesame oil in a blender (not a food processor) until smooth. Season with black sesame seed salt or shichimi-togarashi seasoning to taste.

4 To serve, heat a heavy skillet over medium-high heat and sear the tuna for 5 to 10 seconds on each side. Dice enough watermelon pickle to make ¼ cup and stir this into the diced fresh watermelon. Create a small mound of the mixture on 4 plates and place a piece of seared tuna on top of each. Drizzle each portion with 1 tablespoon of the watermelon emulsion. Garnish with mint leaves and lime crackers.

55

AHI TUNA WITH CAPER RISOTTO

reggiano | aged balsamic | citrus salt

THUNNUS OBESUS

Rich and meaty, bigeye tuna stands up well in this westernized version of Japanese sashimi. Ask for only troll- or pole-caught bigeye, often sold, like yellowfin, under its Hawaiian name "ahi" tuna.

SERVES 4 | SERVE WITH PINOT BLANC, ALSACE

CAPER RISOTTO

3½ cups vegetable stock or water
1 cup dry white wine
¼ cup extra virgin olive oil
1 cup finely chopped onion
1 teaspoon finely chopped garlic
2 bay leaves
1 cup arborio rice
½ cup grated Parmigiano
  Reggiano cheese
3 tablespoons capers, rinsed
1 tablespoon chopped parsley
Kosher salt and black pepper

TUNA

12 ounces finest-quality ahi
  tuna, sliced into thick
  sashimi-style slices
Pinch of Citrus Salt
  (see note below)

GARNISH

Shaved Parmigiano Reggiano
  cheese
2 tablespoons aged balsamic
  vinegar

1 To prepare the caper risotto, bring the stock and wine to a boil in a medium saucepan. Reduce the heat and allow the liquid to simmer.

2 In a wide, heavy bottomed saucepan, heat 2 tablespoons of the olive oil over medium heat and sweat the onion, garlic, and bay leaves until the onion is soft and translucent. Stir in the arborio rice. Add ½ cup of the hot stock to the rice and stir constantly until it is absorbed. Repeat until all the liquid has been added and absorbed by the rice and the rice is al dente.

3 Stir in the remaining oil, the cheese, capers, and parsley. Season with salt and pepper to taste, keeping in mind that the capers are very salty. Spread the risotto out on a baking sheet or shallow dish and allow to cool to room temperature for no more than 15 minutes.

4 To serve, mold a portion of the risotto into a desired shape (round, square, or molded with an ice-cream scoop) on each of 4 plates. Sprinkle the citrus salt over the tuna and place the tuna on the molded risotto. Garnish with shaved Parmigiano Reggiano cheese and drizzle with balsamic vinegar.

NOTE   *At C Restaurant we make our own Citrus Salt and it can be ordered online at www .crestaurant.com. It is also available at specialty food stores across Canada. In Vancouver, look for it at The Gourmet Warehouse, Edible British Columbia on Granville Island, and Stongs Market.*

58

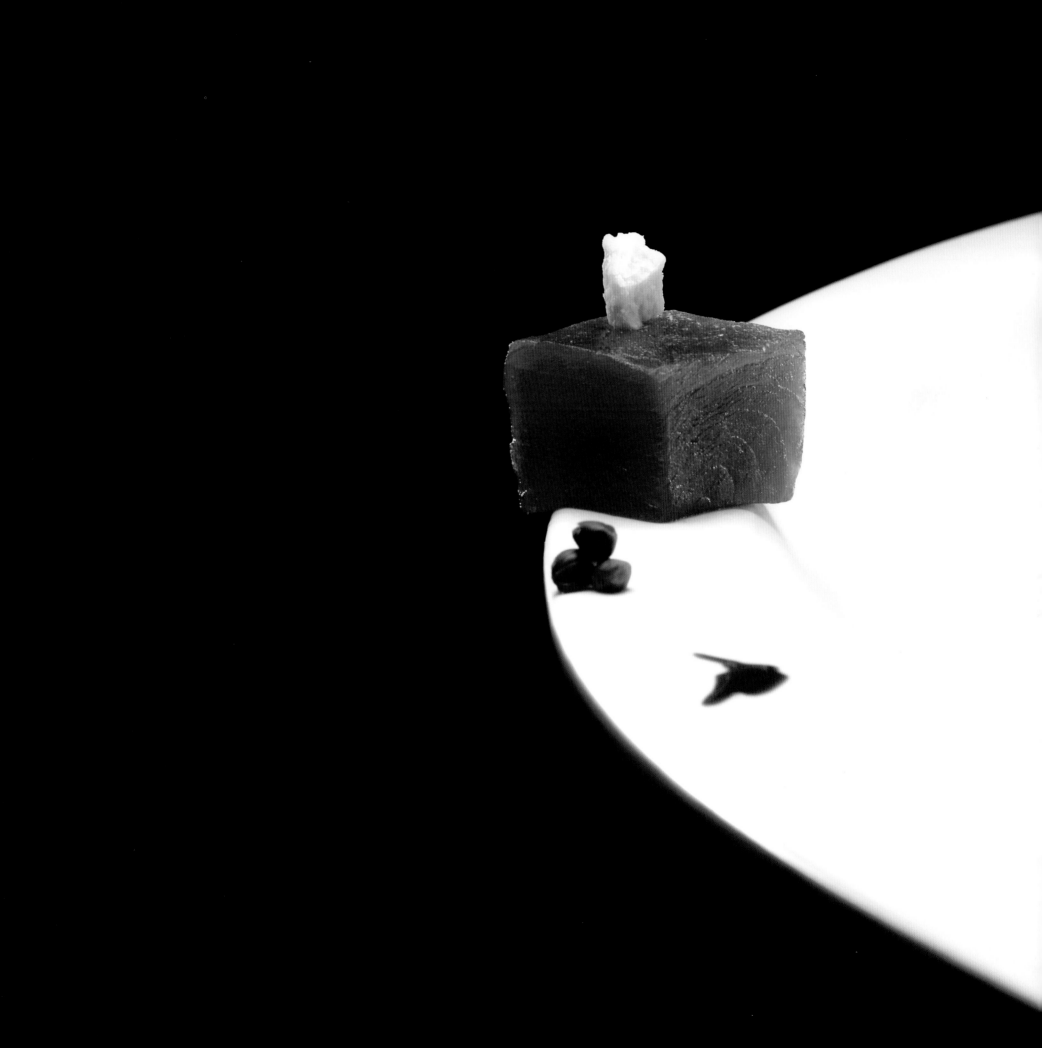

ROASTED B.C. SABLEFISH
wildflower honey glaze | swiss chard

B.C. sablefish is one of my favorite fish to showcase nationally and internationally, and it has always played a key role in our evolution as Canada's leading sustainable seafood restaurant. A very forgiving fish, it is one of the few that tastes better if it is slightly overcooked, so it's ideal for banquets (and first-year apprentices!). In fish markets, it is often labeled as Alaskan black cod, and also sold smoked.

SERVES 4 | SERVE WITH CHARDONNAY, CALIFORNIA

WILDFLOWER HONEY GLAZE
3 tablespoons wildflower honey
1 tablespoon apple cider vinegar
1 tablespoon vegetable oil

ROASTED SABLEFISH
2 tablespoons kosher salt
2 tablespoons granulated sugar
2 cups water
4 pieces (each 4 to 5 ounces)
    fresh sablefish

SWISS CHARD
1 bunch Swiss chard, stems
    removed and leaves coarsely
    chopped
1 tablespoon unsalted butter
Kosher salt and black pepper

1 To prepare the wildflower honey glaze, stir together the honey, vinegar, and oil. Pour half of the glaze into a shallow dish large enough to hold the sablefish in a single layer, reserving the remaining glaze for garnish.

2 To prepare the roasted sablefish, create a brine by dissolving the salt and sugar in the water in a nonreactive bowl. Place sablefish in the brine, then refrigerate for 2 hours to season the fish and firm up its flesh.

3 Preheat the oven to 375°F. Remove the sablefish from the brine and pat dry. Place it, flesh side down, in the dish of wildflower honey glaze and let stand for 15 minutes at room temperature to allow the glaze to soak into the flesh. Remove the sablefish from the glaze and place, flesh side up, in a single layer in a buttered baking dish. Bake for 8 to 10 minutes or until the fish begins to flake.

4 To prepare the Swiss chard, sauté the leaves in the butter just until wilted. Season with salt and pepper to taste.

5 To serve, mound the sautéed chard in the center of 4 plates and lean a piece of the sablefish on each mound. Drizzle with the remaining wildflower honey glaze.

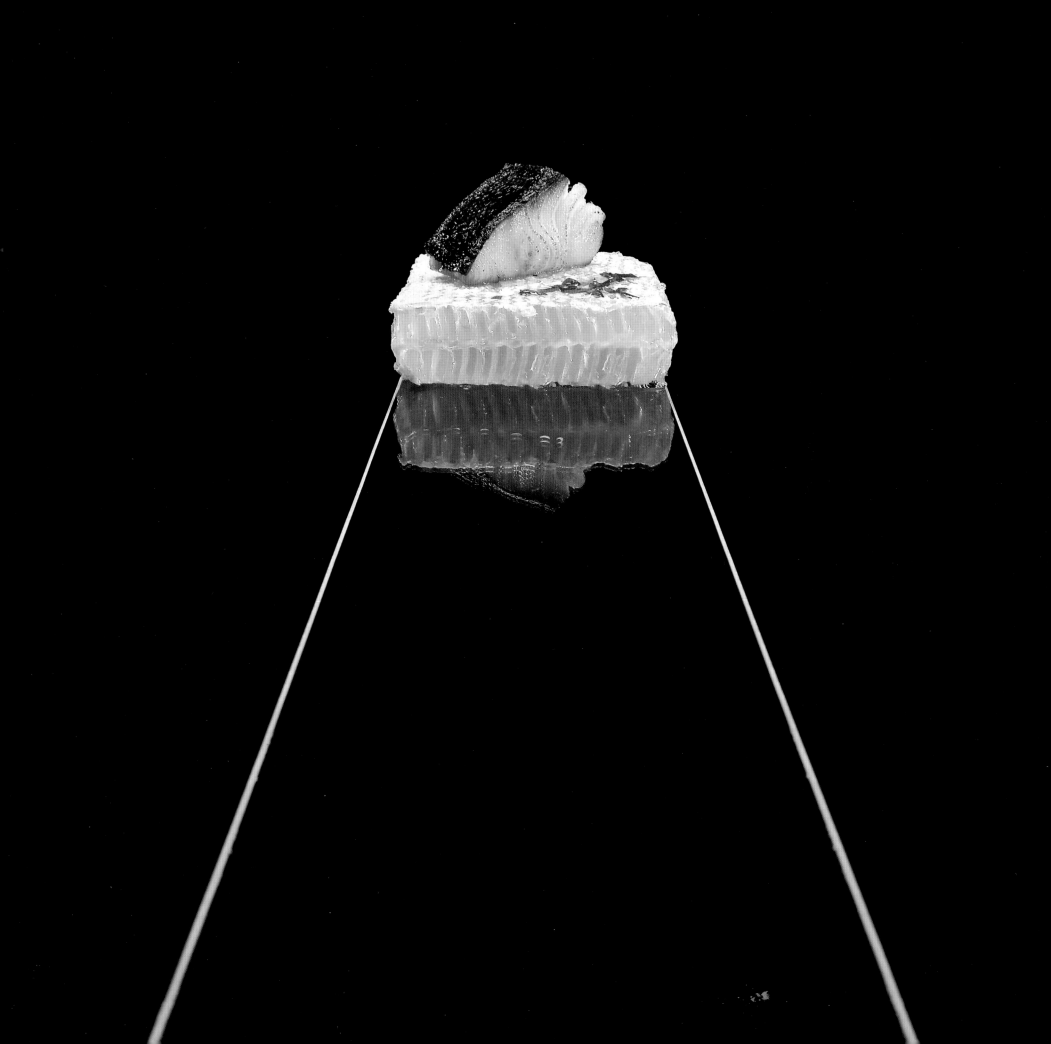

MARINATED BROILED MACKEREL
steamed rice | pickled vegetables

SCOMBER SCOMBRUS (ATLANTIC MACKEREL) | SCOMBER JAPONICUS (SPANISH MACKEREL)

Mackerel, like herring and sardines, have a very high oil content and spoil quickly. Unless you know a fisherman and live within hours of the fishing ground, your best bet is to look for a previously frozen product.

SERVES 6 | SERVE WITH VINHO VERDE

MACKEREL
1 cup Japanese soy sauce
½ cup freshly squeezed
   lemon juice
¼ cup mirin
¼ cup orange-blossom honey
1 pound mackerel fillets
Sesame oil for greasing

GARNISH
3 cups Steamed Seasoned Rice
   (see page 154)
½ cup Pickled Vegetables
   (see page 149), julienned
1 lemon, sliced

1 To prepare the mackerel, stir together the soy sauce, lemon juice, mirin, and honey in a shallow nonreactive dish large enough to hold the fillets more or less in one layer. Add the mackerel fillets and allow to marinate in the refrigerator for 2 hours.

2 Preheat the broiler to high. Brush a shallow roasting pan with sesame oil and place the mackerel fillets, skin side up, in the pan. Broil for 2 to 3 minutes or until the skin begins to darken and caramelize. Remove the pan from the broiler and set aside.

3 To serve, create a tidy mound of steamed rice on 6 plates and drape the mackerel fillets over the top. Garnish with the pickled vegetables and lemon slices.

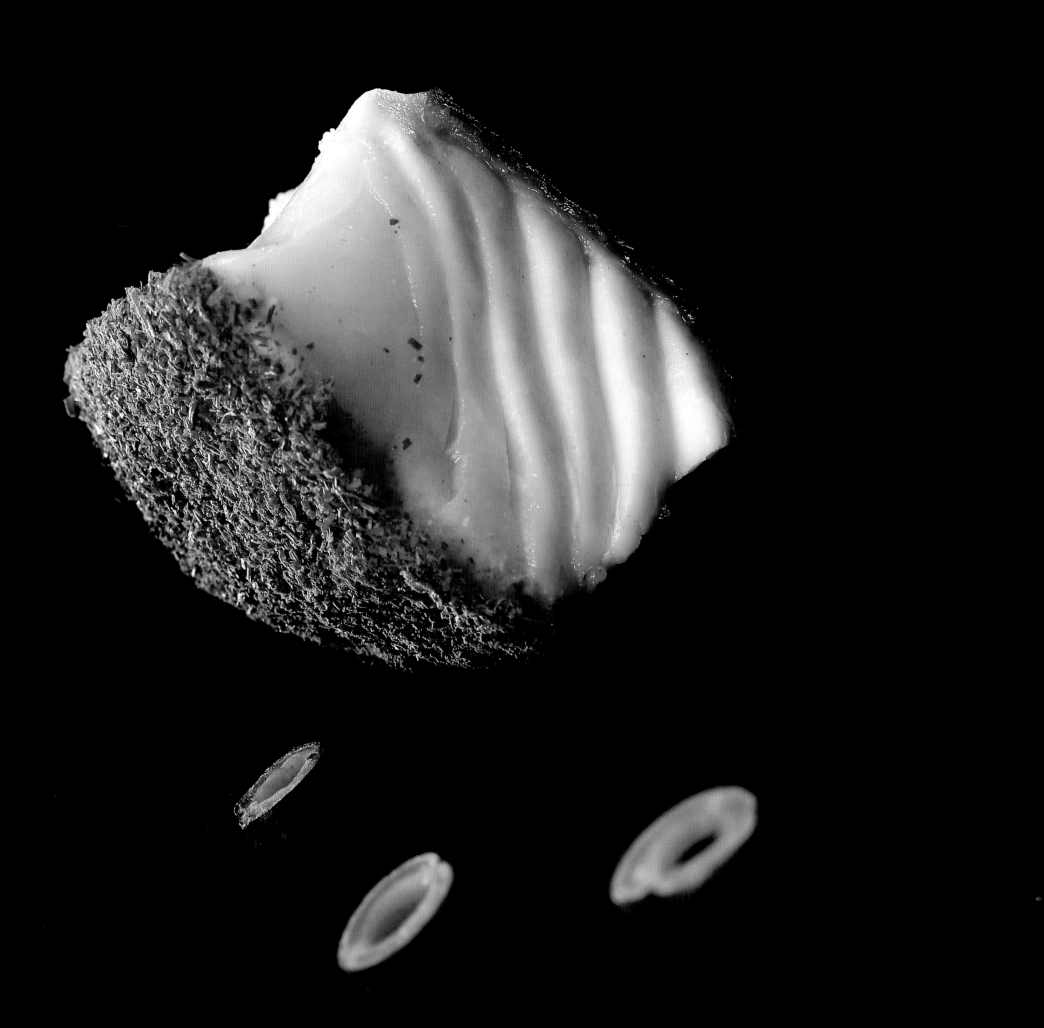

BAKED PACIFIC HALIBUT
green herb crust | summer bean salad

HIPPOGLOSSUS STENOLEPIS

Halibut's large, white flaky chevrons and sweet mild taste make it a popular fish at our restaurants. Available fresh from April to October, halibut is one of the few fish that, at this time, I cannot recommend buying frozen as the freezing process makes it very dry. However, frozen halibut is good for fish and chips, which I am often found to be eating down at False Creek's Fisherman's Wharf from November through March!

SERVES 4 | SERVE WITH WHITE BORDEAUX

GREEN HERB CRUST
1 cup chopped dill
1 cup chopped flat-leaf parsley
¼ cup chopped chives
Pinch of grated lemon zest

BEAN SALAD
2 pounds fresh green or
    yellow beans
2 oranges, peeled and segmented
½ cup kalamata olives, pitted

VINAIGRETTE
1 tablespoon freshly squeezed
    orange juice
1 tablespoon tarragon vinegar
1 tablespoon Dijon mustard
3 tablespoons extra virgin olive oil
Grated zest of 1 orange
1 teaspoon chopped tarragon
Kosher salt and black pepper

HALIBUT
4 pieces (each 4 to 5 ounces) halibut
Extra virgin olive oil
Kosher salt and black pepper

1 To prepare the green herb crust, shock the herbs by blanching them in boiling salted water for 5 seconds. Pour through a fine-mesh strainer, then immediately refresh by immersing the strainer containing the herbs in ice water. Remove the strainer from the ice water and drain well. Purée the blanched herbs in a blender (not a food processor) until smooth, adding a little water if necessary, to achieve a smooth consistency. Avoid leaving the purée in the blender for too long as the heat from the motor will cause it to darken to an unattractive color. Spread the purée thinly on a parchment-paper-lined baking sheet or silicone mat. Place in a warm, dry spot, out of direct sunlight, and allow the herb "paper" to dry for 2 to 3 days.

2 Carefully peel the herb paper off the parchment and grind to a fine powder in a clean coffee or herb grinder, adding the lemon zest as you grind.

3 To prepare the bean salad, blanch the beans in boiling salted water for about 15 seconds, then immediately refresh them in ice water. Drain well. Combine the beans with the oranges and olives, and set aside.

4 To prepare the vinaigrette, whisk together the orange juice, vinegar, and mustard. Gradually add the oil in a steady stream, whisking constantly. Whisk in the orange zest, tarragon, and salt and pepper to taste.

5 Preheat the oven to 375°F. Brush 1 side of each piece of halibut with oil and coat oiled sides evenly with the herb powder. Season with salt and pepper to taste. Place the fish, herb side up, in an oiled ovenproof baking dish and bake for 6 to 7 minutes or until the fish begins to flake.

6 To serve, toss the bean mixture in enough vinaigrette to coat the ingredients evenly. Create a tidy pile of bean salad on 4 plates and lean a piece of halibut against each pile. Drizzle with a little of the remaining vinaigrette.

65

PACIFIC OVEN-ROASTED HALIBUT

parmesan tuile | arugula purée

HIPPOGLOSSUS STENOLEPIS

When purchasing halibut, the flesh should be shiny not dull, and it should be odorless. Don't be afraid to ask to smell the fish before you purchase it, and remember, if you can smell the fish counter before you see it, don't buy anything but vegetables!

Olives and tomatoes tossed with extra virgin olive oil are a wonderful addition to this dish.

SERVES 4 | SERVE WITH CHABLIS

PARMESAN TUILES
1 large wedge Parmigiano Reggiano cheese

ARUGULA PURÉE
2 cups arugula leaves (no stems)
1 to 2 tablespoons vegetable stock
1 tablespoon extra virgin olive oil

HALIBUT
4 pieces (each 5 to 6 ounces) halibut
Kosher salt
1 tablespoon unsalted butter

1 To prepare the Parmesan tuiles, preheat the oven to 350°F. Using a vegetable peeler, shave four or eight ½-inch-wide strips, each about 6 inches long, from the wedge of cheese. Lay the cheese strips in a single layer, and not touching, on a parchment-paper-lined baking sheet and bake for 3 to 4 minutes or until they begin to turn golden at the edges. Let cool on the baking sheet.

2 To prepare the arugula purée, blanch the arugula leaves in boiling salted water for 1 minute, then immediately refresh in ice water. Drain the leaves and purée in a blender (not a food processor) with 1 tablespoon each of stock and oil until smooth, adding a little extra stock, if necessary, to achieve a smooth consistency. Avoid leaving the purée in the blender for too long as the heat from the motor will cause it to darken to an unattractive color.

3 To prepare the halibut, preheat the oven to 400°F. Season the halibut with salt to taste. Melt the butter in a heavy bottomed ovenproof skillet, then place the halibut in the skillet, skin side up. Transfer the skillet to the oven and roast for 6 minutes, depending on the thickness of the fish. Remove the fish from the oven while slightly underdone; the residual heat in the skillet will cook the fish to perfection.

4 To serve, spoon the arugula purée on 4 plates and top with a piece of halibut. Garnish each plate with 1 or 2 tuiles.

WILD COHO SALMON SASHIMI
house-cured roe | wasabi leaf purée

ONCORHYNCHUS KISUTCH

When you think of British Columbia, wild Pacific salmon immediately comes to mind. It has fed our wildlife since time immemorial, it has sustained the people of our First Nations, and it has helped in the evolution of their remarkable culture. The coho is one of five species of salmon and it's a great fish to eat raw. Freeze it first for at least 48 hours to kill any potential parasites. If you can get your hands on fresh salmon eggs, it's also a lot of fun to make your own caviar. There is such a huge difference in taste and quality that once you've tasted your own you will probably never go back to buying it.

Wasabi leaves may be a bit tricky to find, but wasabi sprouts can easily be found at Japanese grocery stores or organic markets.

SERVES 4 | SERVE WITH CHAMPAGNE, ROSÉ

HOUSE-CURED ROE
¼ cup kosher salt
1½ cups water
4 ounces raw salmon eggs

WASABI LEAF PURÉE
1 cup wasabi leaves or sprouts
½ cup spinach leaves

WILD SALMON
8 ounces previously frozen wild salmon, sliced into thick sashimi-style slices

1 To prepare the house-cured roe, dissolve the salt in the water in a nonreactive bowl. Add the salmon eggs and cure them for 4 minutes. Drain and refrigerate until needed. The roe will remain fresh for 1 week in the refrigerator or can be frozen for up to 2 months for longer storage.

2 To prepare the wasabi leaf purée, blanch the wasabi and spinach leaves in boiling salted water for 1 minute then, reserving the blanching water, immediately refresh in ice water. Drain the leaves and purée in a blender (not a food processor) until smooth, adding a little of the reserved blanching water, if necessary, to achieve a smooth consistency. Avoid leaving the purée in the blender for too long as the heat from the motor will cause it to darken to an unattractive color. Pour into a coffee-filter-lined sieve or fine-mesh strainer and allow to drain overnight in the fridge. Discard the water that drains from the purée.

3 To serve, divide the salmon sashimi among 4 plates and place a small dollop of house-cured roe on each piece. Drizzle with the wasabi leaf purée.

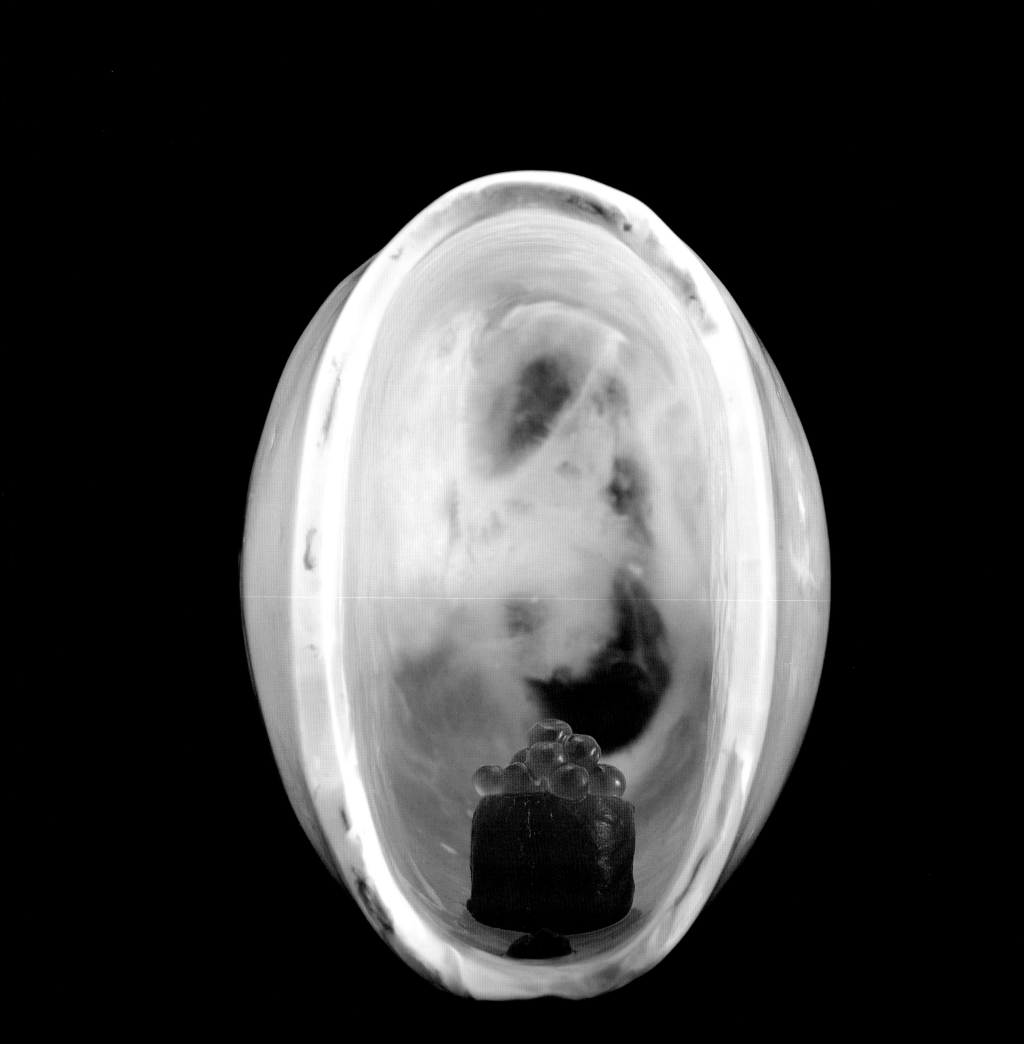

QUINCE-CURED PINK SALMON
fennel | tarragon | anise

In the culinary world, pink salmon is the most misunderstood and under-appreciated of West Coast fish. Constantly compared to the other four species, pinks are seldom treated with the respect that they deserve. The fish have a very short shelf life and, unless you know a fisherman well, it's hard to find a quality fresh product. When I want pink salmon to cook at home, I buy it frozen off the boats at Fisherman's Wharf, or from Iron Maiden Seafoods, a company that does a wonderful job of filleting their pinks. Iron Maiden sells their fish at farmers' markets throughout Vancouver, and it's ideal for this recipe.

SERVES 6 | SERVE WITH PINOT GRIS, NEW WORLD

SALMON
2 sides pink salmon
⅔ cup kosher salt
1 teaspoon anise seeds, ground
¾ cup quince jelly

GARNISH
2 bulbs fennel, trimmed
1 bunch tarragon, coarsely chopped
2 tablespoons extra virgin olive oil
1 tablespoon tarragon vinegar
Kosher salt and black pepper

1 To prepare the salmon, ask your fishmonger to remove the skin, fat, blood line, and pin bones from the salmon, or follow the directions in the Wild Chum Salmon recipe on page 81. Line a very large, shallow baking dish with plastic wrap, leaving an overhang of wrap on all 4 sides. Stir together the salt and anise seeds in a bowl, then sprinkle one-quarter of the mixture in the dish. Brush 1 side of the salmon fillets with half of the jelly and place, jelly side down and side by side, in the dish. Brush the top of the salmon fillets with the remaining jelly and sprinkle with the remaining salt mixture.

2 Fold the excess plastic wrap over the salmon and place another slightly smaller dish on top. Set an object weighing about 5 pounds on top of this second dish. Allow the salmon to cure in the refrigerator for 12 to 24 hours, turning the fish every 8 hours. When the salmon is firm to the touch, remove it from the dish and rinse off the salt mixture. Cutting on an angle, slice the salmon thinly.

3 To serve, using a mandoline slicer, shave the fennel bulbs into thin slices. Toss the fennel with the tarragon. Whisk together the olive oil, tarragon vinegar, and salt and pepper to taste, and toss with the fennel. Divide the fennel among 6 plates. Coil the slices of salmon into rose shapes and place them on the fennel.

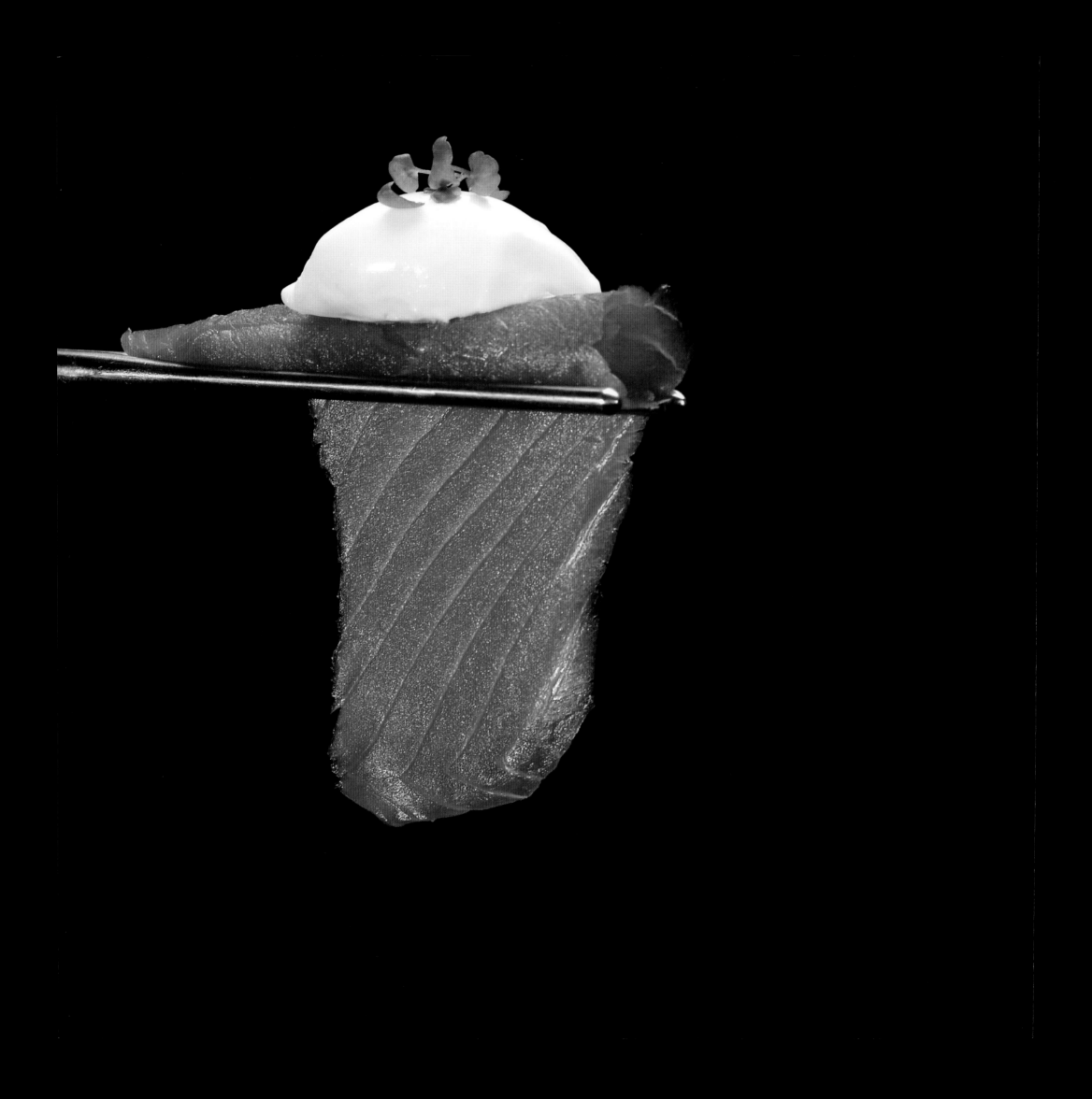

WILD SMOKED SOCKEYE SALMON

crème fraîche sorbet | preserved limes | watercress salad

Knowing a salmon's river of origin is very important as characteristics like taste, texture, and oil content vary from river to river. In keeping with our environmentally sound practices, we always purchase salmon that come from sustainable runs.

SERVES 10 | SERVE WITH SANCERRE

CRÈME FRAÎCHE SORBET
1 cup granulated sugar
1 cup water
Grated zest of 6 limes
½ cup freshly squeezed lime juice (6 to 8 limes)
2 cups Crème Fraîche (see page 112)

SALMON
12 ounces smoked sockeye salmon, thinly sliced

GARNISH
2 cups baby watercress
4 teaspoons finely chopped Preserved Limes (see page 153)

1 To prepare the crème fraîche sorbet, bring the sugar, water, and lime zest to a boil in a heavy bottomed nonreactive saucepan. Simmer this syrup until it is reduced to 1 cup. Strain the syrup, reserving the lime zest for garnish.

2 Whisk the syrup and lime juice into the crème fraîche. Freeze in an ice-cream maker, following the manufacturer's instructions.

3 To serve, create a layer of attractively rolled or folded smoked salmon on a serving platter. Scoop small balls of sorbet on top of each slice of salmon. Garnish the sorbet with watercress and preserved limes.

WILD CHUM SALMON
tip to tail

ONCORHYNCHUS KETA

If you ever have the opportunity to catch your own wild salmon, we recommend you take full advantage of the entire fish. For this recipe we have utilized the liver, heart, rib cage, backbone, skin, roe, and, of course, the flesh of the chum salmon, but any wild salmon of any size will work.

Preparing a great seafood dish actually starts on the boat or at the water's edge. After you have landed your salmon and stunned it with a blow to the head, immediately break the gills by using your fingers or a knife. The fish's heart is still pumping and it will bleed itself out. Scale and gut the fish as you normally would, keeping an eye out for the liver, heart, and roe (if it's a female), and reserve these parts. You can remove any blood left in the stomach cavity by running a spoon along the red blood lines. Rinse the fish and pack it and its offal in ice as quickly as possible.

SERVES 15 TO 20 | SERVE WITH ROSÉ, PROVENCE

1 whole chum salmon
Ingredients for Fish Stock (see page 135); stock to be made using salmon bones and trimmings (see next page)
⅔ cup kosher salt
Vegetable oil for deep-frying
Potato starch for coating

Unsalted butter
Kosher salt and black pepper
Thyme sprigs
Lime Glaze (see page 139)
Seeded and finely diced sweet red pepper (capsicum)
Thinly sliced purple chard
Watercress sprigs

CONTINUED ON PAGE 81 . . .

78

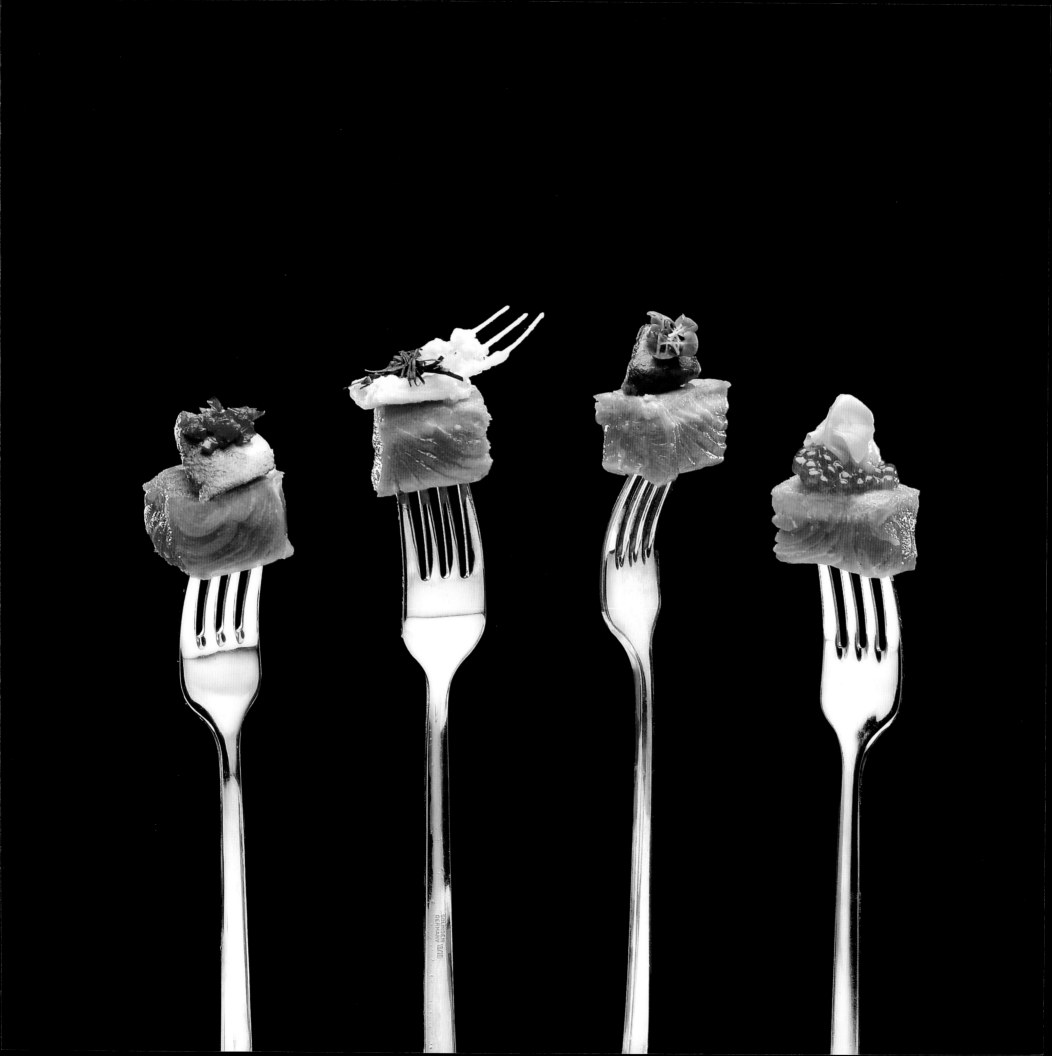

WILD CHUM SALMON (*continued*)

1 To prepare the salmon, with a sharp knife and starting at the head, slice the fish along the backbone toward the tail. Remove 1 side from the salmon. Flip the fish over and repeat the process. To make stock (for use in another recipe), separate the head and tail from the backbone and use these 3 parts, plus any other little bits leftover from preparing the fish. Follow the Fish Stock recipe on page 135. Strain the stock, reserving the backbone but discarding the remaining solids.

2 Remove the rib cage from the sides of salmon by running a sharp thin-bladed knife along the rib bones, starting from where the rib cage was attached to the backbone down toward the belly flap.

3 To remove the skin, place 1 salmon fillet skin side down on a board. Starting at the tail end, run a knife between the skin and the flesh moving toward the head end. Remove the pin bones by pulling them out with tweezers or small pliers. Repeat with the other side of salmon.

4 To prepare the salmon backbone, boil it in salted water for 2 hours. Preheat the oven to 200°F. Drain the backbone and place on a baking sheet. Dry in the oven for about 8 hours or until completely dry. Grind the backbone to a powder in a grain mill. Reserve this salmon-bone salt to season the salmon flesh.

5 To prepare the salmon ribs, dissolve half of the salt in 4 cups water in a nonreactive bowl and brine the rib cage for 1 hour. Remove the rib cage from the brine and cut crosswise into 2- to 3-rib portions. One end of the rib bones will have less flesh than the other. Trim the flesh from that end to create a handle so the ribs are easier to hold. Pour the oil into a deep fryer and heat to 375°F following the manufacturer's instructions. Toss the ribs in potato starch to coat completely and deep-fry the ribs for 90 seconds or until they are crisp and golden brown. Drain the ribs on paper towel.

6 To prepare the salmon skin, remove the scales by running a butter knife or the back of a chef's knife over the skin, scraping from the tail to the head end. Remove the fat and any remaining flesh from the back of the skin. Dissolve the remaining salt in 4 cups water in a nonreactive bowl and brine the skin for 1 hour. Drain well, pat dry, and cut into ¼-inch wide strips. Reheat the oil in the deep fryer to 375°F following the manufacturer's instructions, and deep-fry the skin for 3 to 4 minutes until it puffs up like popcorn. (The skin can be cooled, then refried just before serving.)

7 To prepare the salmon liver, sear it on all sides in butter for about 30 seconds, then season with salt and pepper to taste.

8 To prepare the salmon heart, confit it in butter and thyme for about 40 minutes until tender.

9 To prepare the salmon roe, although the eggs are very tasty eaten straight out of the fish, if you prefer them to have more texture, you can cure them first by following the instructions in the Wild Coho Salmon Sashimi recipe on page 70.

10 To prepare the salmon flesh, cut the sides of salmon into bite-size cubes. Season the salmon with salt and pepper to taste and let stand for 10 minutes at room temperature. To serve, heat a heavy skillet over medium-high heat and sear the salmon for 5 to 10 seconds on each side for medium-rare. Dip the cubes in the lime glaze and sprinkle lightly with salmon-bone salt.

11 To serve, spear the seared salmon cubes on forks and arrange them in 4 portions on a platter. Garnish 1 portion with puffed salmon skin and diced sweet red pepper, the second portion with the salmon ribs and purple chard, the third portion with the seared liver and watercress sprigs, and the remaining portion with cured salmon roe and heart confit.

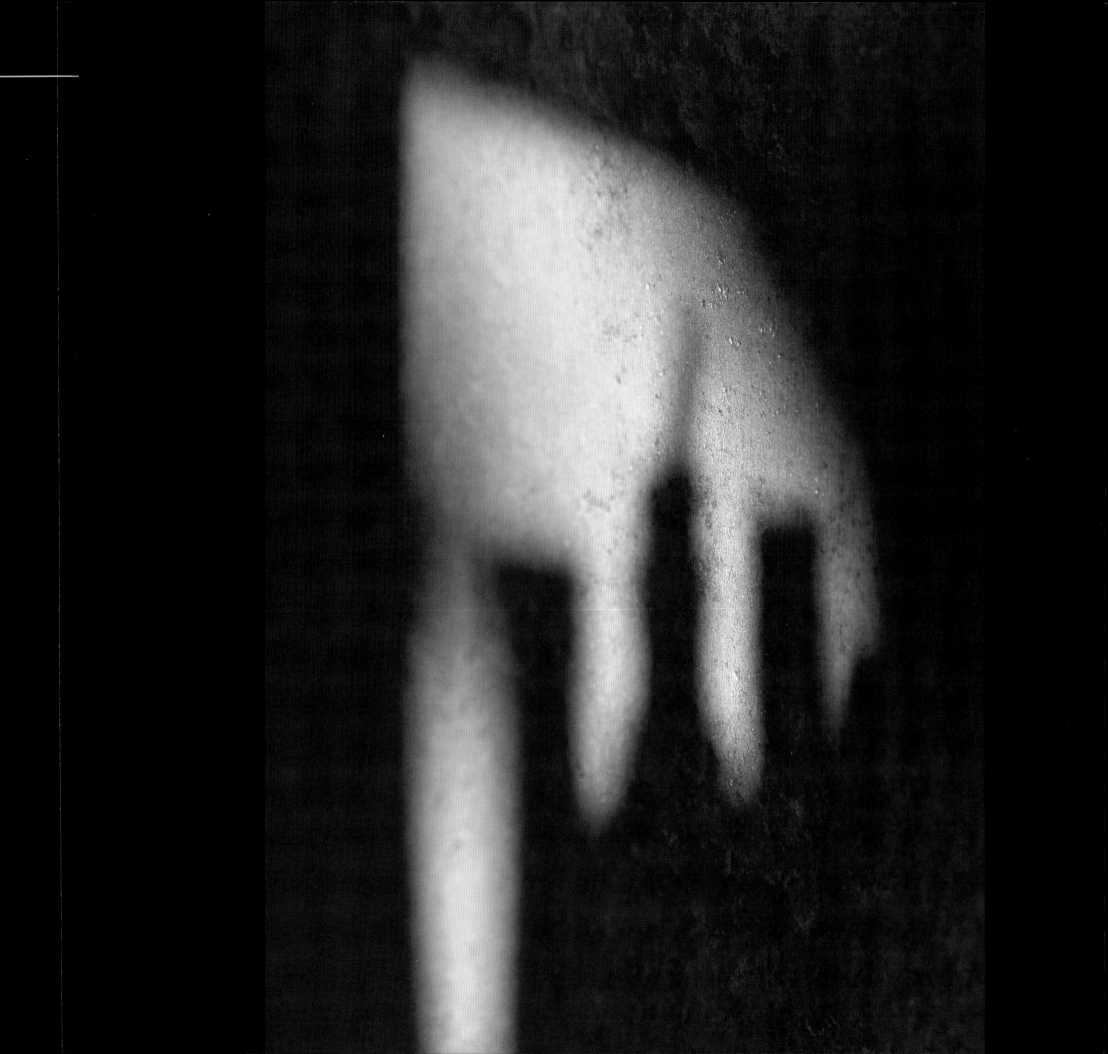

ROASTED WILD SPRING SALMON
spinach gnocchi | saffron cream sauce

ONCORHYNCHUS TSHAWTSCHA

Chinook or king salmon is the largest of the wild Pacific salmon. I find that its oil content makes it one of the most forgiving salmon to cook, and the one least affected by freezing. It is generally our salmon of choice throughout the winter months. If you want a real treat, look for "white spring" or "ivory spring" salmon during the summer months. Though caught randomly up and down the coast, in the summer and fall most white springs are heading up the Fraser to the Harrison River to spawn.

SERVES 4 | SERVE WITH SÉMILLON, HUNTER VALLEY, AUSTRALIA

SAFFRON CREAM SAUCE
½ cup dry white wine
½ cup Mussel Stock
   (see page 146)
2 tablespoons sliced shallot
1 tablespoon tarragon vinegar
1 whole clove garlic
1 bay leaf
1 sprig tarragon
1 cup whipping cream (35%)
Pinch of saffron threads
Kosher salt and black pepper

SALMON
4 pieces (each 6 ounces) wild
   spring salmon
2 tablespoons clarified unsalted
   butter
Kosher salt and black pepper

Spinach Gnocchi (see page 144)

1 To prepare the saffron cream sauce, reduce the wine, mussel stock, shallot, vinegar, garlic, bay leaf, and tarragon in a heavy bottomed saucepan until the saucepan is almost dry. Add the cream and bring to a boil. Strain the sauce through a fine-mesh strainer, discarding the solids. Return the sauce to the saucepan and add the saffron. Reduce the sauce until it is thick enough to coat the back of a spoon. Season with salt and pepper to taste and set aside.

2 To prepare the salmon, preheat the oven to 450°F. Brush the salmon on both sides with butter and season with salt and pepper to taste. Place the salmon on a rimmed baking sheet and bake for 6 to 7 minutes or until medium-rare.

3 To serve, lightly pool the saffron cream sauce on 4 plates. Stack the spinach gnocchi in a tidy pile on the sauce and perch the salmon on top.

PAN-SEARED AGASSIZ FARMED COHO
glazed squash | fresh flageolets | thyme-scented olive oil

ONCORHYNCHUS KISUTCH

To help protect the wild coho stocks, we rely on Bruce Swift and his environmentally friendly, land-locked salmon farm in Agassiz, B.C., to supply us with a sustainable alternative. A great example of integrated agriculture, Bruce's philosophy is a blueprint for the future.

You can also make this recipe using farmed trout with equally delicious results.

SERVES 4 | SERVE WITH PINOT BLANC, NEW WORLD

THYME-SCENTED OLIVE OIL
2 cups extra virgin olive oil
2 bunches thyme
2 bay leaves

GLAZED SQUASH AND FLAGEOLETS
1 cup peeled, seeded, and diced butternut squash, blanched
1 shallot, chopped

1 cup fresh flageolet beans, blanched
½ cup peeled, cored, and diced Granny Smith apple
1 tablespoon unsalted butter
½ cup chicken stock

PAN-SEARED COHO
4 coho fillets (each 6 ounces)
Kosher salt and black pepper
2 tablespoons unsalted butter

1 To prepare the thyme-scented olive oil, heat the oil, thyme, and bay leaves in a saucepan until the oil registers 194°F on an instant-read thermometer. Remove the saucepan from the heat and let the oil stand at room temperature for 5 hours. Strain the oil through a fine-mesh strainer into an airtight container and refrigerate for up to 1 month.

2 To prepare the glazed squash and flageolets, sauté the squash and shallot in 4 teaspoons of the thyme-infused olive oil until the shallot is soft and translucent. Add the flageolet beans, apple, and butter, and cook for 1 minute. Add the chicken stock and reduce until the vegetables are glazed and the chicken stock has a saucelike consistency.

3 To prepare the pan-seared coho, season the fillets with salt and pepper to taste and let stand at room temperature for 10 minutes. Melt the butter in a heavy bottomed skillet over medium-high heat. Place the coho fillets, skin side down, in the skillet and cook until the skin is crisp. Flip the fillets over and cook for about 1 second. The fish should still be a touch undercooked in the center.

4 To serve, mound the glazed squash and flageolets on 4 plates and top each with a coho fillet. Drizzle with a little thyme-scented olive oil.

WHITE & RED MEAT

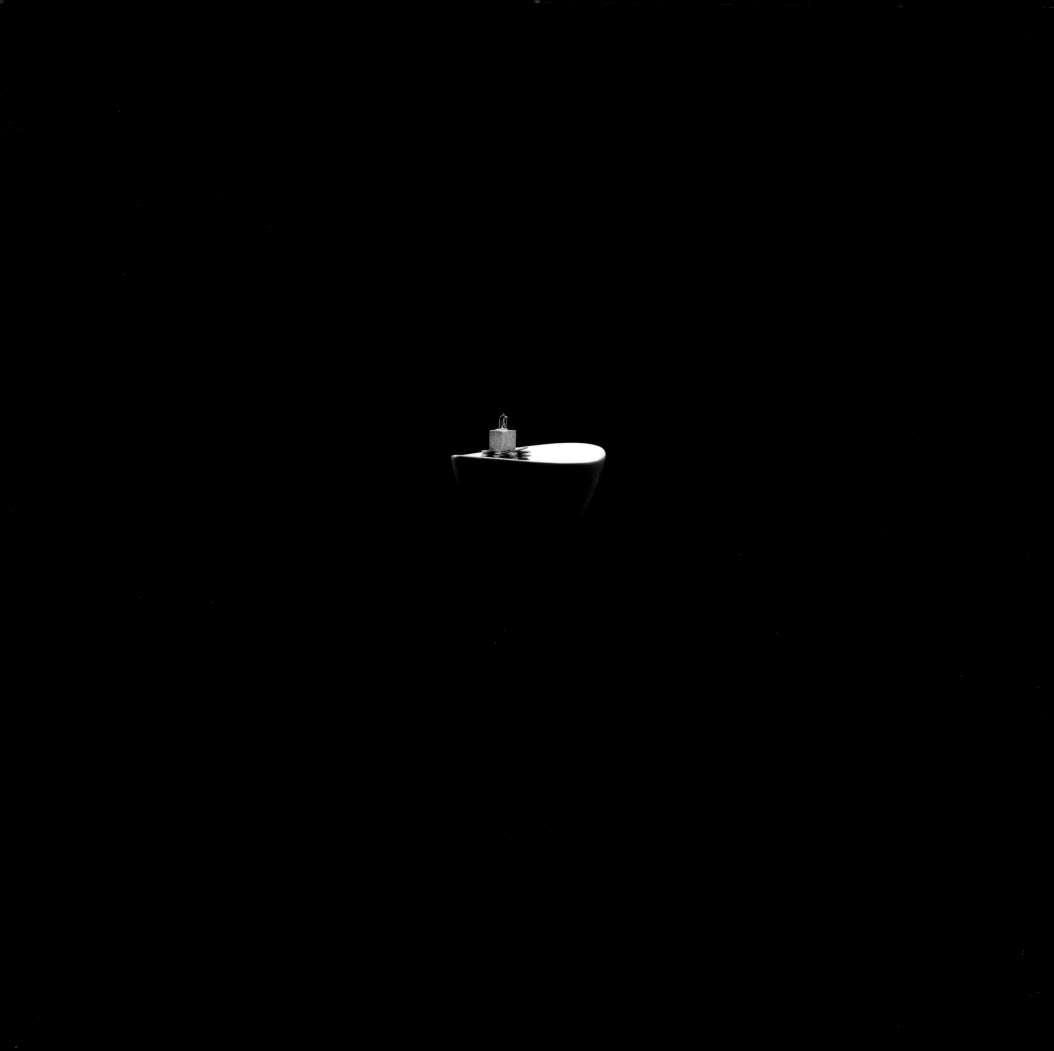

SLOW-ROASTED PORK
damson plums | fresh ginger

Our former chef de cuisine Robert Belcham's love of the pig was the motivator for us to source the quality pork we have in our restaurants today. The hogs we receive from Dirk Keller at Sloping Hill Farm allow us to serve a truly wonderful product and help our young chefs learn how to butcher a whole animal.

When buying pork, look for meat that is a nice rosy pink with bright, white fat. Meat on the bone will have more flavor when it's cooked. Pork wrapped in butcher paper is best, as heat-sealed packaging takes natural moisture out of the meat.

SERVES 8 | SERVE WITH GAMAY NOIR

One 3- to 4-pound piece of
    pork, cut from the shoulder,
    leg, or ribs
6 tablespoons granulated sugar
6 tablespoons kosher salt
7 cups water
1 red onion, sliced
5 cloves garlic, crushed
2 tablespoons sesame oil
2 tablespoons grated fresh ginger

1 tablespoon Pumpkin Spice
    (see page 145)
2 limes, zested and juiced
2 tablespoons seasoned rice
    vinegar
1½ pounds ripe damson plums,
    pitted and chopped
2 tablespoons honey
1 tablespoon molasses

1 In a nonreactive container large enough to hold the pork, dissolve the sugar and salt in the water. Add the pork and brine in the refrigerator for 4 to 6 hours.

2 Preheat the oven to 220°F. In a heavy bottomed flameproof casserole, sweat the onion and garlic in the sesame oil until the onion is soft and translucent. Add the ginger and pumpkin spice and cook for 2 minutes. When the mixture begins to stick to the bottom of the casserole, deglaze with the lime juice and vinegar, scraping the bottom of the casserole clean. Add the plums and lime zest and cook for 2 minutes. Stir in the honey and molasses.

3 Drain the pork and place it in the casserole, turning it to coat with the sauce. Cover the casserole, transfer to the oven, and cook for 3 to 4 hours. Turn the pork over, return the casserole to the oven, and cook, covered, for a further 4 to 6 hours. When the pork is very tender, remove the casserole from the oven and take off the lid. Cover the casserole with aluminum foil and let stand for 20 minutes.

4 Remove the pork to a cutting board. Reduce the cooking liquid in the casserole until it has a saucelike consistency. Carve the pork into slices. Arrange the slices neatly on a serving platter, and drizzle with the damson plum sauce.

POACHED FOIE GRAS
rhubarb sticks | ginger threads

Considered by many to be one of the greatest food pleasures in the world but always controversial, foie gras constantly moves in and out of favor. Fresh or frozen foie gras can be purchased at specialty stores and markets. It should be flesh colored and smooth, with the color consistent throughout, and no discoloration or gray areas caused by oxidation.

SERVES 8 | SERVE WITH QUARTS DE CHAUME CHENIN BLANC

RHUBARB STICKS
1 pound rhubarb, trimmed
2 cups granulated sugar
2 cups water

FOIE GRAS TORCHON
1 pound duck foie gras
3 cups milk
¼ cup Canadian icewine

8 white peppercorns, cracked
1½ teaspoons kosher salt
8 cups water
Black pepper

GINGER THREADS
One 4-inch piece fresh ginger
Peanut oil for deep-frying

1 To prepare the rhubarb sticks, cut the rhubarb stalks crosswise into 6-inch pieces. Using a mandoline slicer, cut the pieces lengthwise into paper-thin slices. Bring the sugar and water to a boil in a saucepan. Reduce the heat and add the rhubarb to the syrup. Poach at a low simmer for 10 minutes or until tender. Remove the rhubarb from the syrup and spread out on parchment-paper-lined baking sheets. Allow to dry in a warm, dry spot for several days until the rhubarb sticks are completely dry and brittle. (This process may be accelerated by using a food dehydrator.) Store in an airtight container.

2 To prepare the foie gras torchon, place the foie gras in a nonreactive container and add the milk. Refrigerate overnight.

3 Remove the foie gras from the milk, discarding the milk, and rinse the foie gras under cold running water. Wrap the foie gras in a tea towel and let stand at room temperature for 30 minutes.

4 Separate the larger and smaller lobes of the foie gras. Place the large lobe smooth side down and, using a sharp knife, cut a slit from the thicker end or top (where the largest vein enters) to the smaller tip, following the large vein. Butterfly the lobe open. Carefully remove as many of the veins as you can. The lobe is very pliable and will easily go back together when you are finished. Follow the same procedure for the smaller lobe.

CONTINUED ON PAGE 95 . . .

93

POACHED FOIE GRAS (*continued*)

5 Bring the icewine and peppercorns to a boil in a small saucepan to burn off the alcohol. Remove the saucepan from the heat and allow the icewine to cool. Strain the icewine, discarding the peppercorns.

6 Place the cleaned lobes smooth side down in a shallow nonreactive dish large enough to hold the lobes side by side and press down on the lobes so they spread to form an even 1-inch layer over the base of the dish. Sprinkle the kosher salt evenly over the foie gras. Pour over the icewine. Lay a sheet of plastic wrap directly on the surface of the foie gras, pressing to ensure there are no air pockets that would cause discoloration. Cover the dish with more plastic wrap to seal it completely. Refrigerate overnight to cure the foie gras.

7 The following day, bring the foie gras back to room temperature. Cut 4 layers of cheesecloth into a rectangle large enough to enclose the foie gras and place the cheesecloth on the counter with 1 long side facing you. Remove the foie gras from the dish and center it on the long side nearest you. Roll up the cheesecloth tightly to enclose the foie gras, forming it into a log 6 to 8 inches long and 3 to 4 inches in diameter. Twist the ends of the cheesecloth to tighten it, compacting the foie gras and forming the log shape. You will know it is tight enough when a small amount of foie gras squeezes through the cheesecloth. Tie the ends of the cheesecloth tightly with kitchen twine.

8 In a large shallow saucepan, bring the water to a simmer. Season the water with salt and pepper and add the cheesecloth-wrapped foie gras. Poach for 1½ minutes. Immediately remove the foie gras from the water and plunge it into ice water to halt the cooking process. Snip the kitchen twine, twist the ends of the cheesecloth to tighten it and retie securely. Hang the foie gras in the refrigerator for 2 days to dry.

9 To prepare the ginger threads, peel the ginger and, using a mandoline slicer, shave it into paper-thin slices. Stack the ginger slices and cut into chiffonade. Pour the oil into a deep fryer and heat to 375°F following the manufacturer's instructions. Deep-fry the ginger threads for about 30 seconds or until crisp and light golden brown. Drain the ginger threads on paper towel.

10 To serve, unwrap the foie gras and slice it crosswise into ½-inch slices. Place the slices on 8 plates and garnish with the rhubarb sticks and ginger threads.

2 tablespoons whipping
cream (35%)
1 teaspoon kosher salt

BRIOCHE SPONGE

1¾ cups (250 grams) bread flour
1 cup milk
1 ounce (30 grams) fresh yeast

8 eggs
1¾ cups (250 grams) bread flour
1 teaspoon kosher salt
Additional unsalted butter
for greasing

CARAMELIZED APPLES

3 tablespoons unsalted butter
3 Granny Smith apples, peeled,
cored, and sliced

1 To prepare the foie gras parfait, bring the Calvados and apple juice to a boil in a small saucepan and reduce it to 1 tablespoon. Remove the saucepan from the heat and let the Calvados reduction cool completely.

2 Blend the foie gras torchon, cream, and salt in a food processor. Pour in the Calvados reduction and purée until smooth. Rub the foie gras mixture through a fine-mesh strainer into a serving dish and refrigerate overnight until set.

3 To prepare the brioche sponge, combine the flour, milk, and yeast until smooth. Refrigerate, covered, overnight.

4 To prepare the brioche dough, cream the brioche sponge with the butter and sugar in a stand mixer fitted with the paddle attachment, until smooth. With the mixer on low speed, add the eggs one at a time, allowing each egg to be incorporated before adding the next one. Replace the paddle attachment with a dough hook and add the flour and salt. Mix the dough until it leaves the sides of the bowl clean and becomes a shiny

mass. Wrap the dough in plastic wrap and refrigerate overnight.

5 Preheat the oven to 350°F. Remove the dough from the fridge and place in an oiled stainless-steel bowl. Cover with plastic wrap and let rise at room temperature for about 2 hours or until the dough has doubled in size.

6 Punch the dough down to remove any large air pockets. Knead the dough into a ball and place in a buttered the pan twice as large as the ball of dough. Let the dough rise at room temperature for a further

2 hours or until it has doubled in size again. Preheat the oven to 350°F. Bake for 35 to 40 minutes or until the brioche is golden brown and sounds hollow when tapped on the bottom.

7 To prepare the caramelized apples, melt the butter in a large skillet over medium heat. Sauté the apple slices until golden brown.

8 To serve, slice the brioche and toast lightly. Spread the foie gras parfait on the toasted brioche and serve with caramelized apples.

ROASTED DUCK BREAST
chokecherry Cumberland | Chinese five-spice

I think duck has been the one constant in my culinary journey, not only professionally here in Vancouver but as I've eaten my way around the world. From elegant restaurants in Paris, Stockholm, and Milan, through street vendors in Georgetown, Bangkok, and Hanoi, to the obscure back alleys of Beijing, you can always find great duck.

SERVES 4 | SERVE WITH PINOT NOIR, NEW WORLD

CHOKECHERRY CUMBERLAND SAUCE
3¼ cups port
¾ cup chokecherry jelly or red- or black-currant jelly
¾ cup freshly squeezed lemon juice
½ cup freshly squeezed orange juice
¼ cup chopped Pickled Kumquats (see page 148), seeds removed

1½ teaspoons cinnamon
1 teaspoon Szechuan peppercorns, ground

ROASTED DUCK BREASTS
4 boneless duck breasts with skin
1 tablespoon Chinese five-spice powder
1 tablespoon kosher salt
Additional kosher salt for garnish

1 To prepare the choke-cherry Cumberland sauce, reduce the port to 1 cup in a heavy bottomed saucepan over medium heat. Add the jelly and stir until melted. Add the lemon juice, orange juice, kumquats, cinnamon, and pepper. Simmer slowly until the liquid has reduced to 2 cups and is thick and glossy. Remove the saucepan from the heat. Serve the sauce at room temperature or cold. (The sauce can be refrigerated for up to 2 months.)

2 To prepare the roasted duck breasts, cut through their skin and fat in a crosshatch pattern with a sharp knife, avoiding cutting into the flesh. Combine the five-spice powder and salt and sprinkle the mixture evenly over the duck breasts. Allow the duck to stand at room temperature for 15 minutes. Heat a large heavy bottomed skillet over medium-high heat. Place the duck breasts in the skillet, skin side down and not touching each other. Cook for about 5 minutes until the fat renders and the skin of the breasts is crispy and golden brown. Turn the breasts over and cook for a further 2 minutes for medium-rare (the breasts should offer some resistance to the touch). Remove the duck breasts to a cutting board and let them rest for 5 minutes.

3 To serve, cut each duck breast into thin slices. Fan the slices out on 4 plates and sprinkle with salt. Drizzle with chokecherry Cumberland sauce.

PORK AND SHRIMP DUMPLINGS

pickled radish | crisp pork rind | ginger vinaigrette

PANDALUS PLATYCEROS (SPOT SHRIMP OR SPOT PRAWN) | PANDALUS BOREALIS (PINK SHRIMP) | PANDALUS HYPSINOTUS (HUMPBACK OR KING SHRIMP) | PANDALUS JORDANI (SMOOTH PINK OR OCEAN PINK SHRIMP) | PANDALUS DANAE (COONSTRIPE OR DOCK SHRIMP) | PANDALOPSIS DISPAR (SIDESTRIPE OR GIANT SHRIMP)

There are six commercially harvested species of shrimp available in British Columbia and they are all better choices than the farmed tiger shrimp that come from southeast Asia. The most sustainable, and the darling of the bunch (due to their high price), are the trap-caught spot prawns we get from Steve Johansen of Organic Ocean Seafood, down at False Creek's Fisherman's Wharf. The season opens in May, and the annual Chefs' Table Society of B.C. Spot Prawn Festival has become the event of the year for Vancouver seafood lovers.

SERVES 4 | SERVE WITH RIESLING, PFALZ, GERMANY, KABINETT

PORK AND SHRIMP DUMPLINGS

8 ounces ground pork

8 ounces shelled B.C. shrimp, chopped

3 green onions (white part only), chopped

1 tablespoon chopped kimchee

1 tablespoon chopped cilantro

1 tablespoon soy sauce

1 tablespoon freshly squeezed lemon juice

2 teaspoons grated fresh ginger

2 teaspoons minced garlic

1 teaspoon kosher salt

Round wonton wrappers

GINGER VINAIGRETTE

3 tablespoons seasoned rice vinegar

1 tablespoon grated fresh ginger

1 tablespoon finely chopped green onion tops

2 teaspoons sesame oil

GARNISH

Grated pickled radish (see Pickled Vegetables recipe, page 149)

Chopped crisp pork skin (available at Asian markets)

Soy sauce

1 To prepare the pork and shrimp dumplings, combine the pork, shrimp, green onions, kimchee, cilantro, soy sauce, lemon juice, ginger, garlic, and salt. Refrigerate for 1 hour to allow filling to set.

2 Lay 10 to 12 wonton wrappers out on a clean work surface. Brush each circle with a touch of water and place 2 teaspoons of the filling at the center of each disk. Fold each in half to create a half moon, then firmly press down on the edges, right up to the filling, removing any pockets of air. Repeat until all of the filling has been used.

3 Let the dumplings rest, uncovered, for 1 hour in the refrigerator. This allows them to dry out around the edges, which helps to form a firm seal. They can then be poached in boiling water or deep-fried in vegetable oil until cooked, about 1 to 2 minutes.

4 To prepare the ginger vinaigrette, stir together all the ingredients in a nonreactive bowl.

5 To serve, arrange the dumplings on a serving platter. Drizzle with the ginger vinaigrette and sprinkle with grated pickled radish and chopped crisp pork skin. Serve piping hot with soy sauce for dipping.

GRILLED BEEF CAP
broccolini | smoked sea salt | beef marrow sauce

Beef cap is a small thin muscle that runs along the outside portion of fat you find on rib-eye steaks or a prime rib roast, with flavor that's superior to the larger rib eye itself. Unfortunately, you probably won't be able to convince your butcher to remove the beef cap from his prime rib! However, any of your favorite grilling steaks (especially those on the bone as these have more flavor) will work in this recipe.

To prepare the bone marrow, soak it in cold, salted water for 8 hours, then drain and poach it in simmering water for 1 minute. Drain it well and slice thinly.

SERVES 4 | SERVE WITH CABERNET SAUVIGNON
OR OTHER BORDEAUX-STYLE RED WINE

GRILLED BEEF CAP
4 pieces beef cap (each 6 ounces) or 4 bone-in grilling steaks
Smoked Sea Salt Flakes (see note below) and black pepper

BEEF MARROW SAUCE
½ cup sliced shallots
½ cup chopped white mushrooms
2 cloves garlic, sliced
1 bay leaf
2 tablespoons unsalted butter
1 cup Cabernet Sauvignon or other Bordeaux-style red wine
3 sprigs thyme
2 sprigs flat-leaf parsley
1 cup Veal Jus (see page 134)
2 tablespoons poached, sliced bone marrow (see note at left)
1 tablespoon chopped flat-leaf parsley

GARNISH
1 bunch broccolini, trimmed
Kosher salt and black pepper
Smoked Sea Salt Flakes

1 To prepare the grilled beef cap, season the pieces with the smoked sea salt and pepper and let stand for 30 minutes at room temperature. (Alternatively, season the beef with regular salt and grill over wood chips to give a smoky flavor to the meat.)

2 To prepare the beef marrow sauce, sweat the shallots, mushrooms, garlic, and bay leaf in the butter until the shallots are soft and translucent. Add the wine, and thyme and parsley sprigs and reduce by two-thirds. Add the veal jus and simmer gently until the sauce is thick enough to coat the back of a spoon and looks glossy. Strain the sauce, discarding the solids. Return the sauce to the saucepan. Just before serving, reheat it over low heat and stir in the bone marrow and chopped parsley.

3 Grill the beef over high heat on the barbecue until cooked to taste. Transfer the beef to a cutting board and let rest for 10 minutes. Meanwhile, steam the broccolini until tender-crisp and season with salt and pepper to taste. Slice the beef and arrange on 4 plates with the broccolini on the side. Drizzle each portion of beef cap with the beef marrow sauce and sprinkle with smoked sea salt.

NOTE *At C Restaurant we smoke our own salt and it can be ordered online at www .crestaurant.com. It is also available at specialty food stores across Canada. In Vancouver, look for it at The Gourmet Warehouse, Edible British Columbia on Granville Island, and Stongs Market.*

BRAISED BEEF SHANK
demi glace

Most of the beef in North America is unsustainably produced. As we move toward more sustainable grass-fed beef, we find that the most effective way to introduce it is by using the braising cuts. Grass-fed beef does not have the same marbling as the meat from beasts fattened on corn in feed lots, therefore it is a bit tougher but still very flavorful. Slow-cooking these tougher cuts allows us to serve a succulent, fork-tender, responsibly produced dish.

SERVES 4 | SERVE WITH SANGIOVESE

BRAISED BEEF SHANK

4 pieces beef shank (each 8 to 10 ounces), cut osso-buco style
Kosher salt and black pepper
3 tablespoons vegetable oil
1 cup chopped onion
1 cup chopped carrot
2 bunches thyme

6 cloves garlic
1 tablespoon black peppercorns
4 bay leaves
1 cinnamon stick
1 cup red wine
6 cups Veal Stock (see page 133)
½ cup pearl onions, blanched
½ cup baby carrots, blanched
½ cup baby turnips, blanched

1 Preheat the oven to 220°F. Season the beef shanks with salt and pepper to taste. Heat a heavy bottomed flameproof casserole over medium-high heat. Add the oil and sear the shanks until browned on all sides. Remove the shanks to a plate. Add the onion, carrot, thyme, garlic, peppercorns, bay leaves, and cinnamon stick to the casserole and sauté for 3 minutes or until the vegetables begin to brighten in color. Deglaze with the red wine. Reduce the wine by half. Return the shanks to the casserole, along with the veal stock, and bring to a simmer. Cover the casserole, transfer to the oven, and cook for 6 to 8 hours or until the beef is very tender.

2 Remove the casserole from the oven and take off the lid. Cover the casserole with aluminum foil and let stand at room temperature for 1 hour. Remove the beef shanks from the casserole and set aside. Strain the cooking liquid into a large saucepan, discarding the vegetables and flavorings. Reduce the cooking liquid until it is thick enough to coat the back of a spoon. Return the shanks to the hot liquid and add the blanched onions, carrots, and turnips. Chill quickly and refrigerate overnight or up to 3 days to allow the flavors to develop.

3 To serve, reheat the braise gently until piping hot. Serve over mashed potatoes.

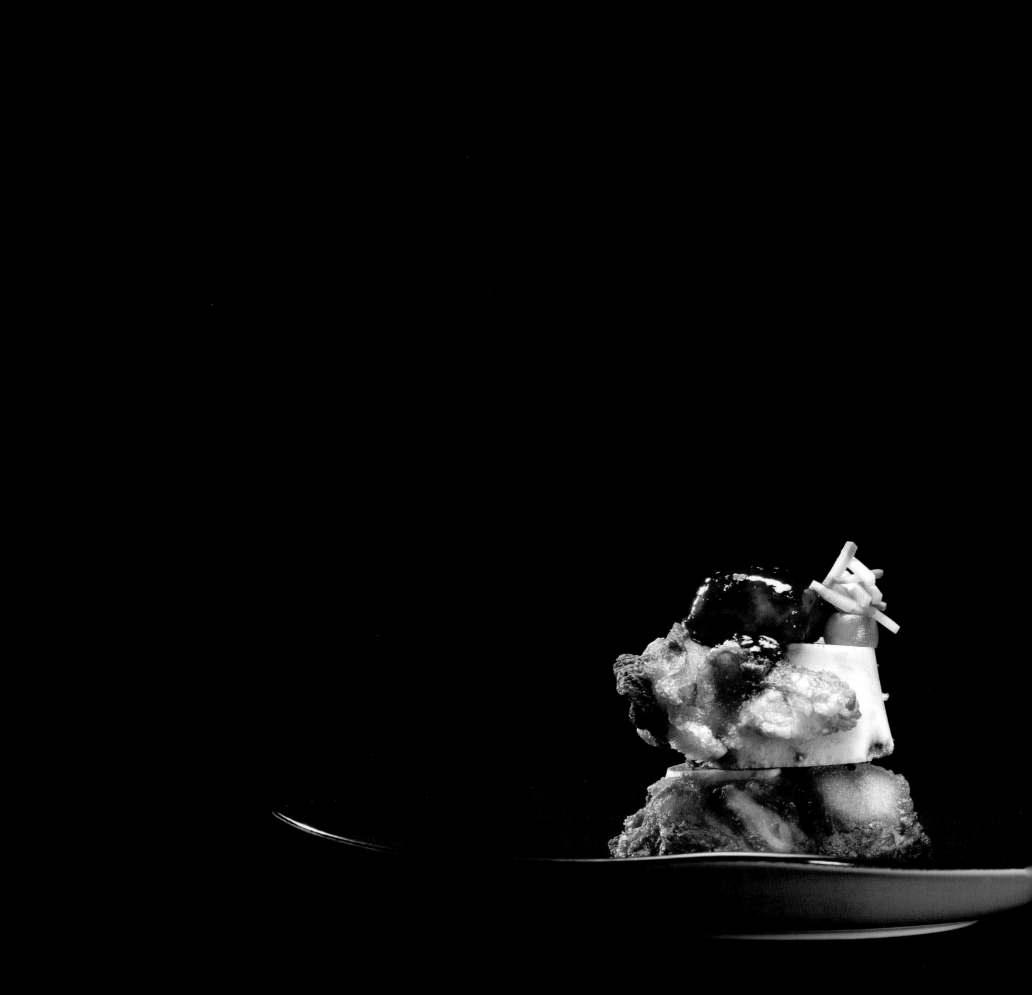

SWEETS

ARMENIAN BREAD
assorted cheese | apple jelly

I love cheese from all over the world, but at home and in the restaurant, I eat and serve mostly local cheese. We have a number of talented cheese-makers in British Columbia, and the best way to nurture them and others is by our support. In time we could begin to see a uniquely regional style of cheese produced here.

SERVES 10 TO 20

ARMENIAN BREAD
Armenian Cracker Straw dough
(see page 38)

GARNISH
Assorted soft and hard cheeses
Apple jelly

1 To prepare the Armenian bread, follow the instructions for making the dough for the Armenian Cracker Straws on page 38.

2 Divide the dough into 4 pieces. Roll out 1 piece of dough to a thin sheet on a lightly floured surface. Carefully transfer to a parchment-paper-lined baking sheet and bake for about 5 minutes or until crisp and golden brown. Let cool on a wire rack, then break into pieces. Repeat with the remaining dough.

3 To serve, arrange an assortment of soft and hard cheeses on a tray with a generous portion of Armenian cracker bread. Serve with apple jelly.

BLACKBERRIES WITH CRÈME FRAÎCHE
lemon tuile

Crème fraîche is wonderful and easy to make. It's a naturally soured cream often used in French desserts, and its slightly sharp flavor livens up everything from soups and sauces to spicy stews. Crème fraîche truly shines on French toast served with pears, pecans, and maple syrup.

If you prefer, the tuiles can be flavored with orange zest, instant coffee granules, grated chocolate, or your favorite spices instead of lemon zest. If you have a kitchen scale, weigh out the ingredients for the tuiles for best results.

SERVES 6 | SERVE WITH LATE HARVEST RIESLING

CRÈME FRAÎCHE
½ cup buttermilk
1½ cups whipping cream (35%)
½ teaspoon freshly squeezed
  lemon juice

LEMON TUILES
¾ cup (100 grams) sifted
  icing sugar
7 tablespoons (100 grams)
  unsalted butter, at room
  temperature

1 teaspoon grated lemon zest
½ teaspoon kosher salt
¾ cup (100 grams) all-purpose
  flour
3 egg whites, at room
  temperature

BLACKBERRIES
3 cups blackberries or other
  seasonal berries

1 To prepare the crème fraîche, mix together all the ingredients in a nonreactive bowl. Cover the bowl with a damp cloth so the cream can breathe while remaining protected. Allow to stand at room temperature for 24 to 48 hours or until the cream has thickened and smells slightly sour. Refrigerate the crème fraîche for at least 24 hours or up to 4 days before using it. If the crème fraîche splits, drain it by placing it in a fine-mesh strainer set over a bowl.

2 To prepare the lemon tuiles, preheat the oven to 350°F. Cream the icing sugar, butter, lemon zest, and salt. Add the flour all at once and mix until well combined. Add the egg whites one at a time, mixing well after each addition to ensure the mixture does not curdle or separate.

3 Place a 2-inch diameter rubber canning seal or your own template design cut out of a plastic yogurt container lid on a silicone mat or a parchment-paper-lined baking sheet. Spoon enough of the batter into the canning seal to fill it. Carefully remove the seal, place it on another part of the mat, allowing room for the tuiles to spread, and repeat the process until the mat is full. Bake the tuiles for 8 to 10 minutes or until they are a deep golden brown. Remove the tuiles from the oven and peel them slowly from the mat. Either drape the warm tuiles over a baking pin or other mold to give them shape and let cool completely, or let cool on a wire rack for flat tuiles. Store in an airtight container for up to 5 days.

4 To serve, dollop the crème fraîche on 6 plates, scatter the blackberries on top, and garnish each plate with a lemon tuile.

WINE LOLLIPOPS
sea salt

Robert Belcham, our former chef de cuisine, is just a big kid inside, and he used to love making lollipops for our customers. Really good wine and really good wine vinegar are essential for these treats.

If you have a kitchen scale, weigh out the ingredients for the caramel for best results.

MAKES 10 TO 12 LOLLIPOPS

WINE REDUCTION
1 cup Cabernet Sauvignon vinegar
½ cup Cabernet Sauvignon
Pinch of fleur de sel
1½ teaspoons citric acid

CARAMEL
½ cup (100 grams) granulated sugar
¼ cup (50 grams) isomalt (see note)
¼ cup (40 grams) liquid glucose
1 tablespoon water

GARNISH
Sea salt

1 To prepare the wine reduction, reduce the vinegar, wine, and salt by about 95 percent to make a thick syrup. Add the citric acid and stir until dissolved. Set the mixture aside. Meanwhile, clean lollipop molds with a cotton ball dipped in rubbing alcohol.

2 To prepare the caramel, combine all of the ingredients in a heavy bottomed nonreactive saucepan. Boil the mixture until it registers 325°F on a candy thermometer. Remove the saucepan from the heat. Allow the mixture to cool until the caramel registers 255°F on the thermometer. Add the wine reduction and stir to combine.

3 Pour the caramel into the prepared lollipop molds or pour small portions onto a baking sheet lined with lightly oiled parchment paper. Insert lollipop sticks into each mold or portion and let cool for about 30 minutes until the lollipops have hardened. Sprinkle each one with sea salt.

NOTE *Isomalt is a sugar substitute made from sugar beets; look for it in baking supply stores.*

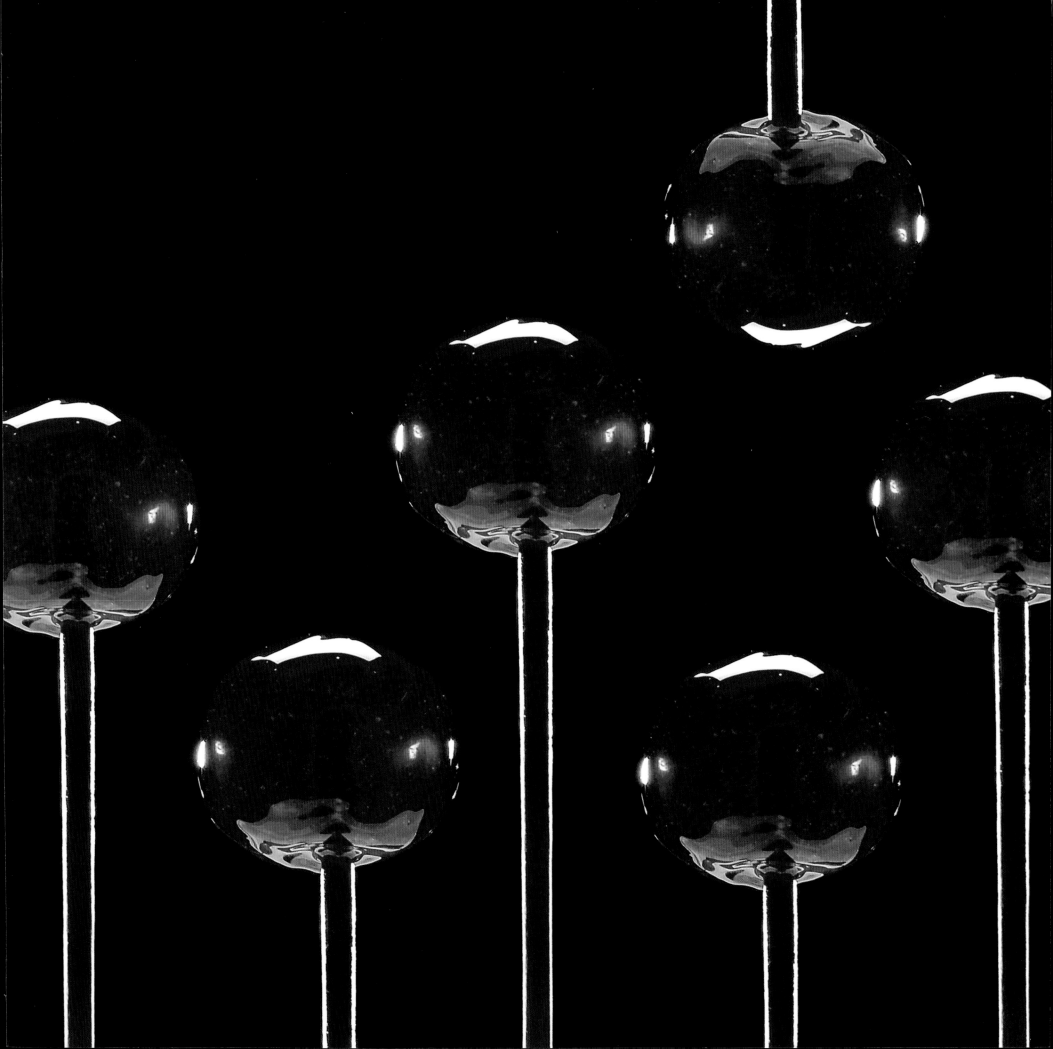

CHILLED ICEWINE JELLY

raspberries | fresh mint

Icewine is the product that made everyone take another look at Canada! After a second sip, the world recognized that we have a credible wine industry here full of passionate and talented individuals, committed to moving our wine programs forward and capable of competing on the global stage.

SERVES 6

ICEWINE JELLY

4 sheets gelatin or 1 tablespoon
   unflavored powdered gelatin
1 bottle (375 mL) Canadian
   icewine

GARNISH

3 cups raspberries
1 bunch mint

1 To prepare the icewine jelly, temper the gelatin sheets by placing them in a bowl of cold water for 2 minutes to soften. Squeeze out the excess water. Stir the soaked gelatin into ½ cup of the icewine in a double boiler until completely melted. Stir the remaining icewine into the gelatin mixture. If using powdered gelatin, put 2 tablespoons cold water in a bowl and sprinkle gelatin over the surface. Let stand for 5 minutes or until puffy. Put the bowl in a small saucepan containing enough barely simmering water to come halfway up the sides of the bowl. Stir for 1 minute or until the gelatin is completely melted. Heat ½ cup icewine just until steaming. Whisk the hot icewine into the gelatin, then whisk in remaining icewine.

2 Pour the jelly into six ⅓-cup molds. Alternatively, pour the jelly into one 2-cup mold so that, when set, you can cut the jelly into desired shapes. Refrigerate for 2 to 4 hours or until set.

3 To serve, run warm water over the bases of the mold(s). Invert the mold(s) allowing the jellies to slide easily onto each of 6 plates or a larger platter. If using a large mold, cut the jelly into 6 pieces and place each on a plate. Garnish the jellies with the raspberries and mint.

BAKED LEMON TART
apricot jelly | chocolate pistachio stick

I love lemon tarts, and not only is this version one of the best but I can actually make it, which can't be said for a lot of other desserts that I have attempted. Another one of Maureen's classical desserts that went on and off the menus at the restaurants for years, this will be the last tart recipe you will ever need.

Look for apricot purée in the frozen-food section of larger specialty food stores, or ask your local pastry store to sell you a 2-pound tub. Powdered apple pectin may be more difficult to find. Look for it online; L'Epicerie (www.lepicerie.com) sells it in the U.S.

If you have a kitchen scale, weigh out the ingredients for the dough for best results.

SERVES 6 | SERVE WITH MOSCATO D'ASTI

APRICOT JELLIES
2 pounds apricot purée
½ cup plus 4⅔ cups granulated sugar
¼ cup powdered apple pectin
2 cups liquid glucose
3 lemons, zested and juiced
1 vanilla bean, split and seeds scraped out

PISTACHIO STICKS
2 cups shelled, salted pistachios, chopped
8 ounces Callebaut milk or dark chocolate

SWEET DOUGH
1¾ cups (225 grams) sifted icing sugar
1⅓ cups (300 grams) unsalted butter, at room temperature
2 eggs
1 teaspoon vanilla
3⅓ cups (500 grams) all-purpose flour
¼ cup (40 grams) cornstarch
Pinch of kosher salt

LEMON TART FILLING
3 eggs
½ cup granulated sugar
Grated zest of 1 lemon
⅓ cup plus 4 teaspoons freshly squeezed lemon juice
⅓ cup plus 4 teaspoons whipping cream (35%)

CONTINUED ON PAGE 121 . . .

BAKED LEMON TART *(continued)*

1 To prepare the apricot jellies, warm the apricot purée over medium heat. Whisk together the ½ cup of sugar and the apple pectin, and add to the apricot purée. Bring to a boil. Stir in the remaining sugar, the glucose, lemon zest and juice, and vanilla bean seeds. Simmer until the mixture registers 223°F on a candy thermometer. Pour into a parchment-paper-lined 9- x 11-inch baking pan. Refrigerate overnight until set.

2 To prepare the pistachio sticks, spread half of the pistachios on a parchment-paper-lined baking sheet. Melt the chocolate in a double boiler until smooth. Spoon the chocolate into a piping bag fitted with a plain nozzle. Pipe lines of chocolate onto the pistachios. Sprinkle the chocolate lines with the remaining pistachios. Set aside until the chocolate hardens.

3 To prepare the sweet dough, cream the sugar and butter in a stand mixer fitted with the paddle attachment. Add the eggs one at a time, beating well after each addition. Beat in the vanilla. In a separate bowl, whisk together the flour, cornstarch, and salt. Add the flour mixture to the creamed mixture all at once and mix slowly just until the flour has been incorporated. Do not overmix. Wrap the dough in plastic wrap and refrigerate for at least 2 hours.

4 Preheat the oven to 325°F. Roll out the dough on a lightly floured surface and fit into a buttered 8-inch tart pan. (If it's too firm to roll out, let it stand at room temperature for 30 minutes.) Place the tart pan on a baking sheet. Line the tart shell with foil and fill with pie weights or dried beans. Bake for about 15 minutes until the edges of the pastry are golden. Remove the foil and pie weights and bake for a further 5 minutes until the center of the pastry is golden. Let cool completely on a wire rack. Reduce the oven temperature to 275°F.

5 To prepare the lemon tart filling, whisk together the eggs, sugar, lemon zest, and juice. In a separate bowl, whip the cream until it just holds its shape. Fold the whipped cream into the egg mixture. Pour the filling into the tart shell. Bake for 12 to 15 minutes or until the filling is just set. Refrigerate the tart for 3 hours or until chilled.

6 To serve, cut the tart into wedges and place 1 wedge on each of 6 plates. Cut the apricot jelly into desired shapes. Garnish each plate with apricot jellies and pistachio sticks.

CRÈME CARAMEL

What more is there to say? This is the perfect crowd-pleasing dessert. It's a simple recipe with few ingredients, yet there are few people who make it well. With no fancy garnishes or exotic sauces to hide behind, a crème caramel needs to be perfect. And, it will be if you follow this classic recipe. Actually, my favorite dessert is crème brûlée, but crème caramel makes a better picture!

If you have a kitchen scale, weigh the sugar for best results.

SERVES 10 | SERVE WITH MUSCAT DE BEAUMES-DE-VENISE

CARAMEL
1½ cups (300 grams) granulated sugar

CUSTARD
2 cups whipping cream (35%)
2 cups whole milk
1 vanilla bean, split and seeds scraped out
1¼ cups (250 grams) granulated sugar
8 egg yolks
3 eggs
¼ teaspoon kosher salt

1 To prepare the caramel, melt the sugar in a heavy bottomed saucepan over low heat. Increase the heat and continue cooking the melted sugar until it becomes amber in color. Pour about 1 tablespoon of the hot caramel into each of ten ⅔-cup custard cups, swirling the caramel up the sides. Place the custard cups in a shallow roasting pan. Preheat the oven to 300°F.

2 To prepare the custard, bring the cream and milk to a simmer with the vanilla bean and its seeds. Remove the saucepan from the heat and allow the flavors to infuse for 15 minutes. Whisk together the sugar, egg yolks, eggs, and salt in a bowl. Whisk the cream mixture into the egg mixture, then strain through a fine-mesh strainer into a pitcher. Pour the custard into the prepared custard cups, dividing evenly. Pour hot water into the roasting pan to come halfway up the sides of the custard cups. Bake the custards for about 50 minutes or until the edges are set but the centers still wiggle slightly when the cups are shaken gently. Remove the custard cups from the roasting pan. Let the custards cool at room temperature for 30 minutes, then refrigerate for about 2 hours or until chilled.

3 To serve, run a knife cleanly around the edge of each custard cup. Invert the custard cups allowing the crème caramels to slide easily onto each of 10 plates. The caramel will run over the custards to form a sauce.

GRAPE SODA

For a tasty alternative to run-of-the-mill soda pops, create your own by making syrup from locally grown fruits. Here, we've used grapes from the Okanagan valley. Served topped up with soda water or sparkling wine, the syrups make a refreshing beverage to serve before, during, or after a multicourse meal.

SERVES 4

4 cups fresh fruit juice, such as grape, blueberry, raspberry, apple, or quince

Granulated sugar
Soda water or sparkling w

1 Simmer the fruit juice slowly in a non-reactive saucepan until it has reduced to ½ cup or less of syrup. Sweeten to taste if necessary. Let cool completely.

2 Divide the syrup among 4 glasses and top up with soda water or sparkling wine.

BASIC RECIPES

SEVEN C'S SPICE BLEND

MAKES ABOUT ⅓ CUP

2 teaspoons caraway seeds

3 whole cloves

3 tablespoons ground coriander

2 tablespoons ground cumin

1 tablespoon ancho chili powder

1 teaspoon ground cardamom

1 teaspoon cinnamon

1 Toast the caraway seeds and cloves in a dry skillet until fragrant, then grind them to a fine powder. Mix with the remaining ingredients and store in an airtight container.

FRENCH DRESSING

¼ cup tarragon vinegar
¼ cup extra virgin olive oil
¼ cup good-quality peanut oil
¼ cup good-quality canola oil
2 teaspoons Dijon mustard
Kosher salt and black pepper

1 Whisk all ingredients in a bowl and refrigerate in an airtight container. The dressing will not stay emulsified and will need to be shaken well before each use.

131

A FEW WORDS ON MEAT STOCKS AND SAUCES

Veal stock is considered to have a neutral flavor and is the most commonly used base for savory sauces. A habit I picked up many years ago at Toronto's Windsor Arms Hotel is to use veal stock as "stage one," or the base, for all my other sauces. In the restaurant's kitchen, we would use the bones or trimmings of other meats to fortify their respective sauces, but use veal stock instead of water to start them off. The contemporary way to make most meat-based sauces in finer restaurants today is to simply take veal or chicken stock, and with the addition of wines, spirits, and/or aromatics, reduce the stock very slowly, straining it every hour or so through cheesecloth or a fine-mesh strainer, until it has a sauce-like consistency. As the liquid reduces it will become a richer-looking color and start to thicken. At this stage, it makes a great sauce that you can enrich by adding butter. If you reduce it too much, it becomes a *glace de viande*, or meat glaze, which is best used to add color and flavor to other sauces.

VEAL STOCK

You can substitute beef, chicken, lamb, or game bones for the veal bones in this recipe. If white stock is needed (a stock without color), omit the tomato paste and carrot.

It takes less time to extract the flavor from the vegetables so we add them halfway through cooking to ensure a cleaner taste. Also, using whole vegetables or ones in large pieces avoids overcooking them and eliminates the "baked bean" flavor that some reduced meat stocks have.

MAKES ABOUT 12 CUPS

5 pounds veal knuckles
2 medium yellow onions, cut in half
2 stalks celery, left whole
1 large carrot, left whole
2 heads garlic, cut in half horizontally
¼ cup tomato paste
4 sprigs thyme
4 bay leaves
1 tablespoon black peppercorns
2 sprigs parsley

1 Rinse the veal bones under cold running water. Place the bones in a stockpot large enough that the bones half fill it. Add enough cold water to the stockpot to cover the bones by 2 inches and bring to a boil. Drain the bones, discarding the water. Rinse the bones again and return them to the stockpot. Add enough cold water to the stockpot to cover the bones by 2 inches and bring to a simmer. Reduce the heat to low and simmer, uncovered, for 4 hours.

2 Skim the stock to remove any fat and impurities that have floated to the surface. Add the remaining ingredients and simmer for another 4 hours, adding more water, if necessary, to ensure the bones stay submerged.

3 Strain the stock through a fine-mesh strainer into a clean stockpot, discarding the solids. Reduce the stock slowly by one-third, skimming the surface occasionally with a ladle to "clean" the stock. Strain the stock through cheesecloth or a fine-mesh strainer. Cool the stock quickly in an ice bath, then refrigerate it for up to 3 days or freeze for longer storage. If you wish, you may further reduce stock by half and use it as a base for meat sauces.

133

VEAL JUS

1 To prepare a neutral fortified sauce reduction, simply reduce veal stock (recipe on page 133) very, very slowly, skimming it occasionally and straining it through a fine-mesh strainer into a clean saucepan every couple of hours, until it has thickened and become a dark, rich jus.

2 As the stock begins to thicken, now would be the time to tweak the jus for specific dishes. For example, to serve it with lobster, add 2 sliced shallots sautéed in butter per cup of jus, deglazing the sauté pan with ¼ cup of brandy per cup of jus. For a beef dish, add whole cloves of garlic and decent red wine (allowing 6 cloves of garlic and ¼ cup of wine per cup of jus).

FISH STOCK

We prefer to cook the vegetables slightly before adding the fish bones for this rich stock, as it takes 20 minutes to extract maximum flavor from the bones, but 30 minutes to do the same for vegetables.

MAKES ABOUT 8 CUPS

1 cup diced white onions

½ cup diced celery

½ cup chopped leek
   (white part only)

2 tablespoons unsalted butter

1 teaspoon white peppercorns,
   cracked

3 bay leaves

1 cup dry white wine

4 pounds good-quality fish bones

1 In a heavy bottomed stockpot, sweat the onions, celery, and leek in the butter for 2 minutes, taking care that the vegetables do not brown. Add the peppercorns and bay leaves and cook for 2 minutes. Deglaze with the white wine and reduce the liquid by half.

2 Add the fish bones and enough cold water to cover the bones by 1 inch. Bring to a simmer and cook, uncovered, for 20 minutes. Remove the stockpot from heat and let stand for 30 minutes.

3 Strain the stock through a fine-mesh strainer lined with cheese-cloth into a clean stockpot, discarding the solids. Reduce the stock slowly until about 8 cups remain, skimming the surface occasionally with a ladle to "clean" the stock. Cool the stock quickly in an ice bath, then refrigerate it for up to 3 days or freeze for longer storage.

LIME CRACKERS

6 cups water
1 cup tapioca starch
4 limes, zested and juiced
1 teaspoon kosher salt
Vegetable oil for deep-frying

1 Combine the water, tapioca starch, lime juice, and salt in a saucepan. Bring to a boil, stirring constantly, for about 5 minutes or until the mixture becomes translucent. Stir in the lime zest. Spread the mixture evenly and very thinly onto a baking sheet lined with silicon or parchment paper. Place in a warm, dry spot for 2 days until it forms a crisp, dry sheet. The sheet will curl and buckle as it dries.

2 Pour the oil into a deep fryer and heat to 350°F following the manufacturer's instructions. Break off pieces of the dried tapioca sheet and deep-fry for 15 seconds or until the pieces puff like a shrimp chip. Drain the chips on paper towel. Bear in mind that the crackers dramatically increase in size as they cook, so test-fry a few pieces first to decide how large you want them to be.

LIME GLAZE

3 tablespoons granulated sugar

1 cup lime juice

1 teaspoon water

¾ teaspoon tapioca starch

1 Dissolve the sugar in the lime juice in a nonreactive saucepan and bring to a boil. Stir together the water and tapioca starch until smooth. Add the tapioca mixture to the lime juice and boil for 1 minute. Strain and let cool.

MAYONNAISE

MAKES ABOUT 2½ CUPS

3 egg yolks

2 teaspoons good-quality
 white wine vinegar

2 teaspoons Dijon mustard

2 cups canola, peanut,
 or light olive oil

2 teaspoons boiled water,
 cooled slightly

Kosher salt

1 Whisk together the egg yolks, vinegar, and mustard in a bowl. Slowly whisk in the oil, one drop at a time. When about half of the oil is added, start pouring in the oil in a thin stream, whisking all the time until the mayonnaise is thick and creamy. Whisk in the water and season with salt to taste. Refrigerate the mayonnaise for up to 1 week.

MUSTARD PAPER

3 tablespoons water

2 tablespoons grainy
    Pommery mustard

1 teaspoon tarragon vinegar

2 or 3 acetate sheets (plastic
    sheets found in office
    supply stores)

1 Purée the water, mustard, and vinegar in a blender (not a food processor). Lay the acetate sheets on baking sheets. Brush the mustard mixture onto the acetate sheets. Place in a warm, dry spot for 1 to 2 days until dry and brittle. Carefully peel the mustard paper off the acetate sheets. Store the paper in a wide, shallow airtight container for up to 1 week. Break into pieces to use as a garnish.

SPINACH GNOCCHI

SERVES 6 TO 8

4 cups spinach leaves (no stems)
2 pounds russet potatoes,
    scrubbed
2 egg yolks
1 cup all-purpose flour
1 tablespoon kosher salt
¼ teaspoon grated nutmeg
Additional all-purpose flour
    for dusting
Unsalted butter for sautéing
Kosher salt and black pepper

1 Blanch the spinach leaves in boiling, salted water for 30 seconds, then immediately refresh in ice water. Drain the leaves and purée in a blender (not a food processor) until smooth. Avoid leaving the purée in the blender for too long as the heat from the motor will cause it to darken to an unattractive color. Pour into a coffee-filter-lined sieve or fine-mesh strainer and allow to drain overnight in the fridge. Discard the water that drains from the purée.

2 Preheat the oven to 400°F. Bake the potatoes for 1 hour or until tender. Beat together the egg yolks and ½ cup of the spinach purée in a bowl. In a separate bowl, whisk together the flour, salt, and nutmeg.

3 Peel the potatoes while they're still hot and pass them through a potato ricer or a fine-mesh strainer. Mound the potatoes on the counter and form a well in the center. Place half of the flour mixture in the well. Pour the egg mixture on top and cover with the remaining flour. Using your fingers, gently mix together the ingredients until a slightly sticky dough forms. Roll the dough in additional flour to dust it.

4 Roll thumb-size pieces of the dough into ½-inch-thick sausage shapes and place on a floured baking sheet until all the dough is used. Cut the sausages of dough crosswise into ½-inch pieces. At this point, the gnocchi may be cooked immediately or wrapped well and frozen for up to 2 weeks.

5 Cook the gnocchi in a large pot of boiling, salted water until they float to the surface. Remove from the water with a slotted spoon and place on an oiled baking sheet to cool. To reheat, sauté the gnocchi in butter over medium heat. Season with salt and pepper to taste.

PUMPKIN SPICE

MAKES 1½ TABLESPOONS

2 teaspoons cinnamon
1 teaspoon ground ginger
1 teaspoon ground allspice
½ teaspoon grated nutmeg

1 Combine all the ingredients and store in an airtight container.

MUSSEL STOCK

MAKES ABOUT 2 CUPS

2 pounds mussels, scrubbed and
    beards trimmed
½ cup diced white onion
½ cup diced leek (white
    part only)
8 whole cloves garlic
1 bunch thyme
1 cup white wine
1 cup white vermouth

1 Heat a heavy bottomed saucepan with a lid over high heat. When it is very hot, quickly add the ingredients in the order they are listed. Cover the saucepan and cook for 2 minutes or until most of the mussels have opened.

2 Strain the stock through a fine-mesh strainer lined with cheesecloth. Discard any unopened mussels. Remove the remaining mussels from their shells and reserve for use in soups, pasta, salads, and other dishes. Cool the stock quickly in an ice bath, then refrigerate it for up to 3 days or freeze for longer storage.

NORI SCONE

This is our most requested recipe, and no cookbook about C Restaurant would be complete without it. Created by our first pastry chef Maureen Seay, our guests have been enjoying this component of our bread selection for more than 10 years.

If you have a kitchen scale, use it to weigh the flour, sugar, and butter for best results.

MAKES 30 BISCUITS

10 cups (1.5 kilograms) all-purpose flour
½ cup (100 grams) granulated sugar
2 tablespoons baking powder
1 tablespoon kosher salt
2 teaspoons baking soda
1 cup sesame seeds
5 sheets nori, cut into small pieces
2 cups (454 grams) cold unsalted butter, grated
5 teaspoons dry yeast
2 tablespoons warm water
4 cups buttermilk
Additional unsalted butter for greasing
Egg wash (1 egg whisked with 1 tablespoon cold water)
Black sesame seeds

1 Preheat the oven to 400°F. In a large bowl, whisk together the flour, sugar, baking powder, salt, and baking soda. Stir in the sesame seeds and nori. With a pastry blender, cut in the butter until the dough resembles coarse crumbs.

2 In a small bowl, dissolve the yeast in the warm water. Make a well in the center of the flour mixture. Pour the yeast mixture and the buttermilk into the well. Mix gently until the dough comes together. Do not overwork the dough or the biscuits will be tough.

3 Roll out the dough on a lightly floured surface to 1 inch thickness and cut into 3-inch diameter biscuits. Place the biscuits on a lightly buttered baking sheet. Brush the tops of the biscuits with the egg wash and sprinkle with the black sesame seeds. Bake for 18 to 20 minutes or until the biscuits are well risen and golden brown.

PICKLED KUMQUATS

This recipe is featured in the Roasted Duck Breast with cumberland Sauce (page 98).

MAKES ABOUT 4 CUPS

1½ cups white wine vinegar

1 cup water

½ cup granulated sugar

2 tablespoons kosher salt

1 cinnamon stick

1 pound kumquats, cut in half horizontally

1 Bring the vinegar, water, sugar, salt, and cinnamon sticks to a boil in a large nonreactive saucepan. Simmer for 2 minutes.

2 Add the kumquats and additional water if necessary so the kumquats are submerged. Return to a simmer and cook for 5 minutes. Remove the saucepan from the heat and let cool completely. Transfer the kumquats and pickling liquid to an airtight container and refrigerate at least 1 week before using. The pickled kumquats can be refrigerated for several months.

PICKLED VEGETABLES

The best vegetables to use for this versatile pickle are any that aren't green, such as onions, squash, beets, cauliflower, carrots, sweet peppers, or radishes. Trim the vegetables and cut them into bite-size pieces.

Prepared vegetables
  (see note at left)
4 cups water
4 cups white wine vinegar
3 tablespoons granulated sugar
3 tablespoons kosher salt
1 tablespoon mustard seeds
2 pods star anise
1 chili pepper

1 Blanch the vegetables in a large saucepan of boiling salted water until they are almost cooked (cooking time will depend on the type of vegetable). Drain well and place in a nonreactive airtight container.

2 Bring the water, vinegar, sugar, salt, mustard seeds, star anise, and chili pepper to a boil in a nonreactive saucepan. Boil for 5 minutes. Pour the hot vinegar mixture over the vegetables. Refrigerate for a couple of days before using. The pickled vegetables can be refrigerated for several months.

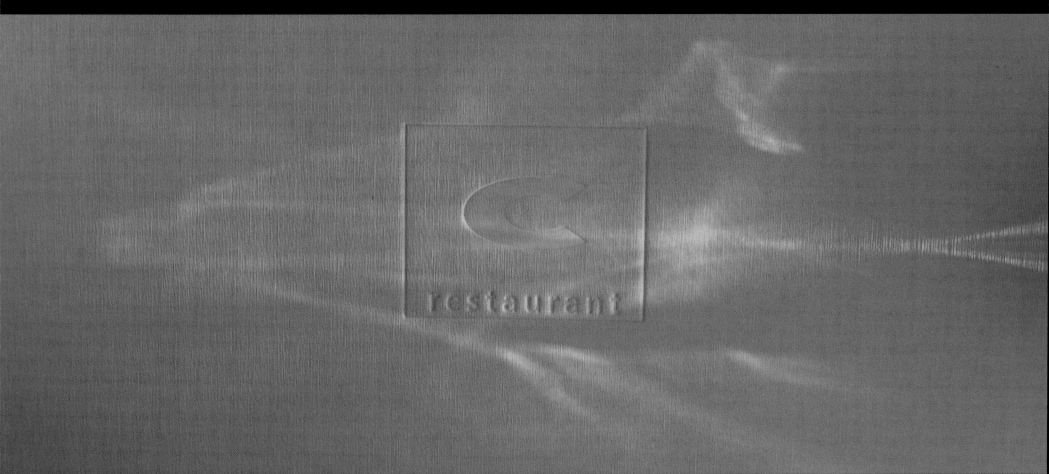

PRESERVED LEMONS

These preserved lemons feature in several recipes in this book. The pickling liquid from this recipe and the one for preserved limes that follows is great drizzled over fish or used in vinaigrettes.

MAKES 48 PRESERVED LEMON WEDGES

6 lemons, each cut into 8 wedges and seeds removed
¾ cup white wine vinegar
½ cup granulated sugar
2 pods star anise
½ cinnamon stick

1 Place the lemon wedges in a large nonreactive saucepan and add enough water to cover them. Bring to a boil. Strain the lemons, discarding the water. Repeat this step 2 more times.

2 Return the lemon wedges to the saucepan. Add the vinegar, sugar, star anise, and cinnamon. The lemon wedges should be submerged by 1 inch. If not, add water to the saucepan. Bring to a boil and simmer for 20 minutes.

3 Remove the saucepan from the heat and let cool. Spoon the lemon wedges, pickling liquid, and spices into a nonreactive airtight container and store in the fridge. The preserved lemons can be refrigerated for several months.

PRESERVED LIMES

This recipe is featured in the Wild Smoked Sockeye Salmon recipe (page 77), but you can also use the liquid for drizzling over fish or in dressings and sauces.

(page 77)

MAKES 12 PRESERVED LIME HALVES

6 limes, cut in half lengthwise and seeds removed
½ cup granulated sugar
½ cup seasoned rice vinegar
½ tablespoon whole allspice berries

1 Place the lime halves in a large nonreactive saucepan and add enough water to cover them. Bring to a boil. Strain the limes, discarding the water. Repeat this step 2 more times.

2 Return the lime halves to the saucepan. Add the sugar, vinegar, and allspice. The lime halves should be submerged by 1 inch. If not, add water to the saucepan. Bring to a boil and simmer for 10 minutes.

3 Remove the saucepan from the heat and let cool. Spoon the lime halves, pickling liquid, and spices into a nonreactive airtight container and store in the fridge. The preserved limes can be refrigerated for several months.

153

STEAMED SEASONED RICE

If you have a rice cooker, simply follow the manufacturer's directions; if not, use the method here.

MAKES ABOUT 8 CUPS

3⅓ cups sushi rice
4 cups water
One 2-inch piece kombu
 (Japanese seaweed)
Seasoned rice vinegar

1 Wash the rice until the water runs clear. Drain well and place in a large saucepan with the water and kombu. Bring to a boil and remove the kombu.

2 Cover the saucepan tightly and boil for 2 minutes. Reduce the heat to medium and boil for 5 minutes. Reduce the heat to very low and simmer for 10 to 12 minutes or until all the water has been absorbed by the rice. Remove the saucepan from the heat and let stand for 5 to 10 minutes. Gently stir in rice vinegar to taste.

154

¼ tsp	1 mL
½ tsp	2.5 mL
1 tsp	5 mL
1½ tsp	7.5 mL
2 tsp	10 mL
1 Tbsp	15 mL
4 tsp	20 mL
1½ Tbsp	22.5 mL
2 Tbsp	30 mL
¼ cup	60 mL
⅓ cup	80 mL
½ cup	125 mL
⅔ cup	160 mL
¾ cup	185 mL
1 cup	250 mL
1¼ cups	310 mL
1⅓ cups	330 mL
1½ cups	375 mL
1¾ cups	435 mL
2 cups	500 mL
3 cups	750 mL
3¼ cups	810 mL
3½ cups	875 mL
4 cups	1 L
5 cups	1.25 L
6 cups	1.5 L
7 cups	1.75 L
8 cups	2 L
12 cups	3 L
2 gallons	8 L

1 oz	30 g
2 oz	60 g
3 oz	100 g
4 oz	125 g
5 oz	175 g
6 oz	200 g
8 oz	225 g
9 oz	250 g
10 oz	300 g
12 oz	350 g
1 lb	454 g
1½ lb	750 g
2 lb	1 kg
3 lb	1.5 kg
4 lb	1.8 kg
5 lb	2.2 kg

¼ inch	6 mm
½ inch	1 cm
1 inch	2.5 cm
2 inches	5 cm
3 inches	8 cm
4 inches	10 cm
6 inches	15 cm
8 inches	20 cm

194°F	90°C
200°F	95°C
220°F	104°C
223°F	106°C
250°F	120°C
255°F	124°C
275°F	140°C
300°F	150°C
325°F	160°C
350°F	180°C
375°F	190°C
400°F	200°C
450°F	230°C

CANS

28 oz	796 mL

y   fish   rest

INDEX

159

ROBERT BELCHAM

This book would not be the same without the creative input of our former chef de cuisine Robert Belcham. His enthusiasm for the artistic presentation of the photos, and his belief in quality ingredients above all, shine through on the pages of this book.

MAUREEN SEAY

Robert's wonderful wife and the former pastry chef of C Restaurant, for her patience and, more importantly, for her dessert contributions!

MICHELE KAMBOLIS

A local artist whose kind words and persistence kept the procrastinators in our group moving forward with the project. Her editing and observations helped us bring shape to the book.

RACHEL AUSTIN ATTIE

A talented chef, and Hamid's better half, Rachel was lucky enough to be the first person to see the original draft. She helped clean up the recipes so that they read in English.

LUKE KENNEDY

Our former sous chef and the man running the kitchen at C Restaurant while Belcham and I worked on the photos. Luke was set with the task of testing the recipes for the first round.

HAMID ATTIE

There would not be a book without the fabulous images of this very talented photographer. His photos were in fact the inspiration for the book. Hamid was a pleasure to work with—he brought professionalism and humor to every shoot. We greatly appreciate his patience with our obscure presentations, and his confidence in our direction and approach to the food photography.

SARA BANNERMAN

In charge of our wine program at C Restaurant and Nu Restaurant + Lounge, Sara is behind the wonderful wine pairings in this book.

LORIE AND SIMON SCHELLE

For providing the plates and wonderful risen art pieces that (literally) provided the base for our inspiration.

QUANG DANG

Our chef de cuisine for his hard work and dedication to the restaurant and for elevating the quality of our expanded catering operations.

THE STAFF AT C RESTAURANT

The entire staff at C Restaurant, who have (knowingly or not) played a key role in the production of this book by continuing to meet the needs of our customers. And to the great management we have had over the years—Cate Simpson, Peter Bonder Rod, Tim Pittman, Tom Doughty, Shannon Ronalds, Leonard Nakonechny, Annette Rawlinson, Kim Cyr, and Martin Repicky.

THE FACILITATORS

Everyone at Whitecap Books, who were a pleasure to work with, making the whole experience of publishing this book a rewarding one.

—*Robert Clark & Harry Kambolis*

ROBERT CLARK
Executive Chef

Ever cognizant of the delicate interconnected web of quality, diversity, sustainability, and market demand that surrounds the seafood industry, Robert Clark is a firm believer that, as a chef and a trendsetter in food, not only should he be responsible about the food choices he makes, he can also inspire change in the industry to which he has devoted his life.

Born in Montreal and raised on the Gaspé Peninsula, Clark's passion for cooking began at a young age, and in his grandmother's kitchen. Clark also credits his early forays as an avid angler and forager along the fertile, salmon-abundant York River near his family home for his well-honed appreciation for fresh fish.

During his early career, he apprenticed and worked with some of Canada's top chefs, including Jamie Kennedy, Nigel Shute, Michael Bonaccini, Mark Thuet, John Higgins, and Nils Kjelson. In 1997, when Harry Kambolis decided the time was right to open Vancouver's definitive seafood restaurant, he recruited Clark to join his team as chef de cuisine. Within the year, Clark was promoted to the position of executive chef. Since then, Clark's leadership in the C Restaurant kitchen has been the key to the restaurant's success as a prime dining destination in Vancouver, a restaurant that has won awards for its distinctive cuisine and wine lists as well as raves from critics across the continent.

HARRY KAMBOLIS
Owner

Although most people go with the flow, Harry Kambolis's mission is to do the exact opposite. With the opening of Raincity Grill in the early '90s, Harry started building countless relationships with both local farmers and producers of quality ingredients by serving what would soon be known as seasonal "Pacific Northwest cuisine." He also supported local British Columbian wines long before it was in vogue. By offering only wines from B.C. and the American northwest, and by having the largest selection of "wines by the glass" anywhere in North America, Harry developed a successful business model that many have since emulated.

The opening of C Restaurant in 1997 to critical acclaim was another opportunity for Harry to demonstrate his commitment to celebrating regional bounty. The restaurant's mandate was to look beyond the typically homogenized selection of seafood available on menus around the world, by sourcing out and introducing about 60 local varieties of the highest quality, all of which were locally harvested. By promoting overlooked and previously underutilized local species, C paved the way for many mainstream white-tablecloth restaurants in Vancouver today. Further, in what was once considered a "cursed location," C has flourished for over ten years as the leading seafood restaurant in Canada.